Standing Firm

Copyright © 2015 by Gerald C. Anderson Sr.

All rights reserved. No part of this book may be used or reproduced by any means, graphic, electronic, or mechanical, including photocopying, recording, taping or by any information storage retrieval system without the written permission of Gerald C. Anderson Publishing except in the case of brief quotations embodied in critical articles and reviews. This is a work of fiction. All of the characters, names, incidents, organizations, and dialogue in this novel are either the products of the author's imagination or are used fictitiously.

Because of the dynamic nature of the Internet, any Web addresses or links contained in this book may have changed since publication and may no longer be valid. The views expressed in this work are solely those of the author and do not necessarily reflect the views of the publisher, and the publisher hereby disclaims any responsibility for them.

Gerald C. Anderson Publishing – May 2015
10800 Nautica Place
White Plains MD 20695
ganderson@geraldcandersonsr.com
www.geraldcandersonsr.com
Facebook: www.facebook.com/geraldcandersonsr
Twitter: @geraldcanderson

I would like to take a minute to thank the below listed contributors to Standing Firm. Without their assistance this book would not have been possible.

Standing Firm Contributors:

Editor, Author Susanna K. Green, sweetnectarpublishing@yahoo.com

Reviewer/Assistant: Kanika Johnson

Cover design: Mad House Design Inc, madhousedesigninc@gmail.com

Cover photography by Anthony Cole

Cover models (Pictured from left to right):

Andra Richardson, http://andrarich.com, andra.richardson1@gmail.com
Renata Mikae, booking.renatamikae6@gmail.com Twitter: @renatamikae6
Sharosia McCall, ancarri@mail.usf.edu

Book Trailer Actor/Actresses:

Penny… Andra Richardson, http://andrarich.com, andra.richardson1@gmail.com
Raine…Renata Mikae, booking.renatamikae6@gmail.com Twitter: @renatamikae6
Damien…Greg Grist, gmgphotoflim@gmail.com
LaJuan…Shante Ashmeade, shanteashmeade5@hotmail.com

Book Trailer Make Up:

April Davis Mua, redlipsreview@gmail.com

Book Trailer Producer

Omar Richardson, O Richardson Designs,
orichardsondesigns@gmail.com

Public Relations: Bobby Foxworth, brenajones.bj@gmail.com

Event Planner (DC): Leslie Saint-Julien,
 Leslie@lesliesaintjulien.com

Dedication – Johnnie B. Sweet

Standing Firm is dedicated to my grandmother, Johnnie B. Sweet. My grandmother is one of many who have suffered through domestic violence but she survived and was an inspiration to writing this novel. She was first and best singer I ever knew. I love you Johnnie B. Sweet.

Prologue

The annual meeting took place in a dark and dreary European country. These powerful men gathered to discuss the transactions of the previous year and what expectations and moves they planned to make in the upcoming year. These men not only ran countries, they ran the world.

The leader stood up, "We have done some great things over the past year. We have achieved success in every walk of life and in every nation around the globe. However, the music industry needs a shot in the arm. We need someone electric; someone the people can identify with and love; someone charismatic and charming, with a pure heart."

The leader sat down and the music industry representative stood up, "We believe we have just the person. She's a young, talented lady from a fine family. We have been watching the Davis family for the last decade. We've made certain moves to divide the family in order to achieve our goal of signing this young talent. Our representative will be on the church grounds next Sunday to offer the oldest sister a contract. We believe going through the oldest sister is the best method because the one we really want will become extremely jealous and will sign with us. We do not expect the oldest sister to sign."

The leader said, "Are you placing this in Mr. Black's hands?"

"Yes, Mr. Black has been briefed about his past behavior and I'm assigning one of our best operatives to assist and watch over him and the young lady," he said.

The leader's voice became transparent, "Good, we expect to see some great results. We have been given permission to do whatever we may, except we cannot take the life of any Davis member. If we do she will be released from her contract and we will have to pay the price. Therefore, ensure Mr. Black understands."

"Yes sir."

Chapter 1

Penelope "Penny" Davis was the lead singer of her church choir and destined to be a legend. Her voice was magnificent and stirred deep in the souls of those who listened to her sing.

Today was the first Sunday of the month and people often came from miles around to hear a song by Penny. She took her place in front of the crowd and prepared to sing. The music blared as she listened for her cue. She was a true professional and no matter what the situation was, she knew what to do.

"Time has come, for a change. Time has come, to speak his name...Jesus! Jesus is his name..." At the high note of the song the crowd shouted with joy. Some stood while others shouted. Many quietly emerged themselves in the words of the song but all of them were touched by the words, the music and sound of Penny's beautiful voice.

Penny felt the power of the song and only she could deliver it. She noticed her father as tears flowed down his face. He was always proud of his oldest daughter but this Sunday and this song was particularly special to both of them. Penny didn't let him or her family down.

A year ago on this day, Diane Davis went home to be with the Lord. It was a sorrowful day for the Davis family as their mother's bout with cancer had come to an end.

Penny and her two sisters loved their mother and it hurt deeply when she passed. The Davis family felt the loss of a loved one before but it was when Penny and Nya were toddlers. Their baby brother passed away at a young age but they were too young to remember it. The loss of their mother was much different because they were adults and could feel the hurt more deeply.

Penny sang her mother's favorite song and everyone in the service knew it. The musicians were friends of Penny's and the Davis family and the choir loved them all which made it special to all of them.

Penny prepared hard for this moment and now she delivered it with a true passion for her mother and the Lord she so fervently loved. The entire sanctuary stood, praising the Lord in the way that pleased them. Again, Penny had done her mother proud.

At the end of the song she held her hands up high to give honor to her mother. Tears ran down her face and the memories of her mom flooded her mind. Flashes of happy times, sad times and all of them in between raced through Penny's mind. Moments later her sister, Nya put her arm around her and guided her off the stage. She thought of resisting but didn't.

Behind the sanctuary and in the choir room, Penny cried profusely. The emotions of the moment overwhelmed her and she needed time to recover. Nya brought her some much needed water.

Nya and Penny got along well as sisters and Nya was always there for Penny, "Thanks Nya, you always know what I need when I need it."

Nya smiled, "You know I got you girl."

Cornelius Davis was the father of the Davis sisters. He was a strong man but missed his beautiful wife. He was standing at the doorway. Penny saw him through her tears and managed a smile. He came over and hugged both of them tightly.

Penny said, "I love you, Daddy."

Cornelius hugged her even tighter, "I love you too, baby. I love you so much. Your mother would be so proud of you. I'm so proud of you."

"I know she was up there listening, Daddy. I just know she was."

Lorraine "Raine" Davis was the baby of the family and considered the wild one of the Davis house. Her coffee colored skin and long jet black hair made her the dream of every man in the city. She was tall and slender. Today she wore an orange dress with African decorations down the middle. She looked like a queen.

Raine sashayed into the room as if she owned it, "Well, didn't we just put on a show for the crowd." She waved her hands in the air and smiled, "Aaaaamen."

Penny had nothing but love for Raine but most of the time she was annoyed with her to no end. Raine was very pretty but Penny believed all the Davis women were pretty. She felt Raine had to be the best at everything and now on the day she dedicated her song to their mother Raine again tried to be the center of attention.

Penny scowled at her baby sister, "Not now Raine!"

Raine smiled, "If not now, when?"

She cocked her head to one side and hugged her big sister. No matter how much they conflicted with each other, Raine still loved and respected her sister, "You know I'm just teasing with you."

Penny managed a smile, "Yeah girl. You know how to work a nerve."

Raine said, "I learned from the best…you."

Cornelius stepped in, "Okay ladies, we don't need any conflict on today of all days."

Raine hugged her daddy, "Daddy, I'm being good. You know I made your favorite banana pudding for dinner tonight. Aren't you happy"

Cornelius smiled, "Yeah baby, I'm very happy."

Penny cringed. Her dad had been played by Raine again. She couldn't stand how everyone just bought into Raine's sweetness and the batting of her eyes. She got her way with anything. Now in Penny's moment she had found a way to make it about her again.

Penny walked passed them. Her dad grabbed her hand, "Penny, you okay?"

Penny's head dropped, "Yes Daddy, I'm fine." She stared at Raine for a second and walked out the room.

***

After church Penny stayed around and congregated with other members of the service. She was talking to one of the choir members when her high school classmate, Derrick came up to her with a friend. Penny hoped he wasn't trying to set her up with this guy because she wasn't in the mood.

Derrick said, "Penny this is Damien, Damien Black and he's an AR from Fresh City records."

Penny's eyebrows rose to meet her forehead, "Hi, how are you?"

Damien smacked his lips, "I'm fine, you have a very gifted voice and I was so impressed with what I heard today. I want to sign you right now, how about it?"

Penny's face was frozen, "Really? I don't know."

Damien continued, "Look, I know it's a bit much to get with so fast but trust me, from what I heard you have the talent to make it to the top. Here's my card. Let's do this."

Penny replied, "I'll..."

Raine startled her sister, "Hey, you haven't heard me blow yet. You should listen to me before you sign her. I'm just saying."

She put her arm around Penny and smiled at the men.

Penny stared at her, "Will you give it a rest? You're just a baby."

Derrick stepped in, "Damien, this is Raine, Penny's youngest sister. She's very talented as well."

Raine said, "Excuse me…as well? Damien, I'm the best in the family; and, I'm twenty-two years old…not a baby."

Damien smiled and shook Raine's hand, "Well it's nice to meet you pretty lady and might I add you're wearing that dress."

He stared her up and down while Penny's face filled with despise. Damien continued, "Wow...so I could sign two sisters? That would be great."

Penny grabbed Raine's arm, "No, that wouldn't. She's too young and she's going to finish college and get her degree. That's what our mom would've wanted."

Raine yanked her arm from Penny, "You don't speak for me. I speak for myself, thank you. And how do you know what mom would've wanted?"

She turned toward Damien, "If you want to hear a real singer let me know." Raine turned and walked off.

Penny shook her head, "I'm sorry but she's too young. I have your card and I'll let you know. We are talking gospel music right?"

Damien shrugged his shoulders, "Music is music so it doesn't matter."

Penny put her hand on her hip, "It does to me. If it's not gospel, then I'm not interested."

Damien gently grabbed her by the arm, "Come on, don't make that decision so fast. I know you're a Christian but music is not a sin. You can still be a Christian and sing rhythm and blues music. There's nothing wrong with that. Shoot we can even throw a couple of gospel tracks on your album." He paused, "Look at stars like Aretha, Whitney, Patti LaBelle and Tina Turner...they all started in church. You can too. You can be the next big star."

Penny smiled because she was being nice, "Thank you and I do realize that but I'm a woman of God and I don't want to leave my service to the Lord to sing in the world. That's just my opinion and it counts more than anyone else's."

Damien said, "Just give it some thought. I think you can be a bigger star than all of them."

"Thank you, I will give it some thought," said Penny.

She walked off towards her car. She truly gave it some thought and wondered if it would be okay to leave church and sing rhythm and blues music. As she got in her car, she saw Raine had made her way back over to them. She knew Raine wouldn't let it go. It had been her dream to sing on the big stage all her life and now this man was offering her a deal.

A couple of times in the past Raine hinted about leaving home and heading to California to try and make it in the music industry. The one thing that stopped her was their mom. Diane had a powerful control over Raine.

Raine respected her mother and couldn't manipulate her like she could her father.

Now their mother was gone and the door was open for Raine to do what she wanted. Penny knew she would manipulate their father and get her way.

Penny couldn't allow it. She suspected something wasn't right with Damien. She didn't like his mannerisms. It sickened her to see Raine talking to Damien and Derrick. She knew what her sister was up to and she knew she couldn't control her. No one could control Raine Davis anymore.

Penny drove away from the church to get ready for their family dinner in honor of Diane Davis. Everyone made something delicious to bring to the dinner. She was going to change and finish her dish for the dinner.

The long ride home gave her a chance to contemplate signing with Damien Black. Her gut told her that this man was not the one but she would do some research on him to see what kind of man he really was.

She knew she couldn't just tell Raine that he wasn't a good man; she needed to have some proof. She needed something to support what her spirit was already telling her about him.

She prayed, *"Father in Heaven I call on your name. I need you father. I need your guidance. Father this man has come in and wants to sign me and my sister to a record deal. Father, you know I want to sing to your glory and not to the worlds. I don't care about being famous, I care about being saved.*

Father, you know my sister is ambitious, head strong and determined to do what she wants to do. Please touch her spirit and show her the right way to go. Show her that she needs to stand on your word and not give in to the world.

Lead me father, guide me father, and show me the way. Signing a record deal can get my sung words to millions of people but will they hear me or your word. Without you at the head of our lives, we are nothing.

I give it all to you father. I turn this situation over to you. In your wonderful son Jesus' name I pray, Amen."

Chapter 2

Raine Davis was the baby of the Davis family and played it to her advantage. She used her beauty to get her way and her siblings didn't like the way she behaved. They loved her because she was their sister but they had issues with some of her actions.

Damien said to Raine, "I feel a connection with you. Your sister doesn't understand what we can do. If you can sing as good as she can then we can make money baby." He paused as Raine stared into his eyes, smiling, "Maybe I can bring you down to the studio and hear you sing. If I like what I hear, maybe we can do that contract."

Raine replied, "That sounds good to me and trust me you will love what you hear. I got skills. When can we set that up?"

"How about tomorrow evening; we can have dinner and then hit the studio? I'm telling you baby I feel something here." He put his hands on her shoulders and smiled.

Raine was excited but she tried to hold it inside. She couldn't wait to get to that studio and make her dream come true. All the times she thought of running off to California and trying to make it but couldn't because her mother wouldn't let her. Now her dream came to her doorstep.

Raine didn't care for Damien touching her but she didn't want to upset him either, so she allowed it, "That sounds like a plan to me. I can meet you at LaRusso's on 50th Street."

Damien giggled, "Meet me? Baby when I court a star I don't meet them. I'll send a limo to pick you up. That's how we do it at my label."

Raine was surprised. Except for her prom night, she had never rode in a limo, "Well that would be nice except I don't want my judgmental family to see that. My dad would never let me get in it. So let's just meet there at 7, okay?"

Damien nodded, "Okay, we'll do this your way but at some point you'll probably have to leave them and their judgments behind. You know what I mean?"

"I know exactly what you mean. I'm grown but they still want to treat me like I'm twelve. I still live with my dad so I do have to respect him. Now if you don't mind I have to go to my family's dinner. Since my mom passed we gather every Sunday for dinner. Trying to keep the family together and strong, you know?"

He reached out, took her into his arms and kissed her on the cheek, "That's cool; I'll see you tomorrow sweetheart."

Raine felt a chill go up and down her spine. This time he kissed her on the cheek and she really didn't like it. She had a boyfriend and no one ever kissed her but him and her dad but again she didn't want to lose this opportunity so she allowed it, "Okay, bye."

She quickly turned and walked away from Damien. She could feel him staring at her backside as she walked away. It made her smile but it also made her uncomfortable. She thought that if she could make this man like her she could use him to get to the top of the music world but at some point she would have to let him know that she loved Jay and no one could come between the two of them.

She wondered if she would let Damien go further if it meant getting a record deal. She quickly dismissed the thought, hoping to never have to go there.

Raine got in her car, started it up and thought, *'The first thing I can do with my money is buy me a better car! This piece of crap will be trashed, never to be seen again.'*

She drove off pass Derrick and Damien. She waved and smiled seductively as she sped by and headed home.

She couldn't get her mind off the music industry. Her entire family was musically talented but she was the only one who wanted to do more than sing in the local church. She thought they were wasting their lives away at the local level but that wasn't going to let happen to her. She was going to be a star.

***

For the last year dinner at the Davis' home has been an event. Sometimes it was fun, other times it was filled with drama. No one really knew what to expect each week but today was a special day as all of them missed their mom.

Their father had suffered greatly over the past year without his childhood sweetheart. They met in the sixth grade and always loved each other. When Diane Davis passed it hurt Cornelius so much that he had to be hospitalized.

Raine loved her father and no one else could control the young twenty-two year old but him. But unlike her mom, her dad had limits. She could get away with doing things with her dad that she could never get away with, with her mom. She was truly daddy's little girl. Since birth, her siblings resented that but she didn't care. The middle sister, Nya was most affected by Raine.

Penny and Nya were born a year apart and Nya was the baby for four years until Raine came along. Their mother always said that Nya was jealous because Raine took her place.

Everyone in the family always said how cute little Raine was and Nya secretly resented it. For years the two of them never got along and today would be no different.

As Raine pulled up to the house, she didn't know how she was going to tell her father that she met with an AR man from a rhythm and blues record label. She knew it would break his heart.

Her father was a devout Christian man and didn't want his children doing anything outside of Christianity. Raine believed she could sing rhythm and blues and still be a Christian. She believed that all music came from God and it wouldn't matter.

She walked in the house where everyone else was already waiting on her. She could tell they were annoyed at her late arrival. The room went silent as she walked in the door. She smiled inside, knowing that they were talking about her but she didn't care. She walked up to her dad, "Hey Daddy...sorry I'm late."

"It's quite alright, baby girl," Cornelius motioned to everyone, "Come on everyone, let's pray and eat."

This dinner was special so all of Raine's aunts, uncles and cousins were there as well.

All of the food was on the table and it smelled good. Raine and her sisters were great cooks. Their mother taught them almost from birth how to cook.

She took her customary place at the table between her father and Penny. She loved sitting by her father.

Cornelius said, "Everybody take a hand and bow your head. Father, thank you for bringing my family together once again; we're not perfect by no means Father but, bless all of us to see the good in each other over the bad."

"Father, bless my children, my brothers, sisters and my nieces and nephews to make the right decisions in their lives. I trust that you will guide them in the way they should go. Protect them from all hurt, harm and danger, both seen and unseen."

"Father, bless the food we're about to receive for the nourishment of our bodies and bless the hands that prepared it. In your wonderful and magnificent son Jesus' name...Amen."

Everyone said Amen and got their food. The atmosphere was tense. The small talk was present but it was clear that it was only a means to disguising what everyone really wanted to talk about.

Bryan, Raine's cousin said, "Penny, girl you tore that song up today. I know auntie is up in Heaven still loving it."

Penny smiled, "Thanks Bryan; all I thought about was momma, hoping she was happy with it."

Nya added, "Girl everyone loved that song. You got skills, you should make a record."

Everyone looked at one another. That was the subject they didn't want brought up. Raine quietly picked over her food, not wanting to participate in the small talk. Instead she ate and played with her four year old cousin who sat at the next table.

Cornelius turned to Raine, "Raine, who is this Damien guy?"

Raine didn't want to answer the question but she couldn't lie knowing Penny wouldn't cover for her.

She smiled, "Daddy, he's an AR guy from Fresh City Records."

Cornelius pressed Raine, "What did he want with you?"

Raine looked at Penny. She knew her sister had blabbed to all of them.

Raine sighed, "He's interested in signing me and Penny to a record deal."

She added Penny's name to it hoping it would soften the blow a bit. She looked at her father expecting his coarse judgmental stare.

Instead Cornelius looked down at his plate. Raine was unsure what to say.

Penny jumped in, "Daddy, I told him 'no' for both of us but you know...I don't speak for Raine."

She got up from the table and went into the kitchen.

Raine hated her oldest sister sometimes. She took her father's hand. He looked up at her and smiled. She smiled back at him, batting her eyes, hoping to diffuse the situation. That usually worked with her father and she wasn't afraid to use it.

His curiosity was obvious, "What did you say to him?"

Raine looked down.

Cornelius continued, "You know I raised you to be a Christian woman and I don't want you singing for the world."

Raine looked sad, "But Daddy..."

Cornelius raised his hand, "You know your mother would not approve."

Raine said to herself, *"Not the mother excuse again. I am so tired of hearing what mom would have approved of or not. God help me get out of here!"*

"Daddy, just because you sing R&B doesn't mean you don't love the Lord and it doesn't mean that I'm not a Christian woman. It's a job like bagging groceries at the local store. You don't say anything about someone who does that."

Cornelius looked at his baby girl, "You will not be surrounded by likeminded people. When you are surrounded by others who do not believe as you believe you can succumb to what they believe. Raine, I love you. You are my youngest child and there is nothing I will not do for you. Please turn away from this man. He is not your friend."

"Just because he's not in church; come on, Daddy? That's being judgmental. That's what I hate about you Christians. If you ain't in church you're a bad person; come on."

"'You Christians'; so you're not one of us now?"

"That's not what I meant, Daddy."

Nya spoke up, "Raine, you are barely twenty-two years old. At least, let one of us go with you to see what this man has to say."

"Yes, I am twenty-two and that means I'm grown. I don't need anyone to take me by the hand."

She stood up but her father grabbed her by the hand and pulled her back down, "I'm not finished young lady."

She loved and respected her father so she eased back down. Her father looked at her, "If you do this, you do it without my blessing."

He stood up and left the table without finishing his food. This was an action Cornelius rarely, if ever, did. He never left the table without finishing his food, so Raine knew he was upset.

Tears began rolling down her face. Her family tried to comfort her. Raine blocked out their comments. She didn't want to hear what they had to say. She didn't believe any of them respected her because she was young.

One by one, everyone got up and walked into the kitchen or the living room. Raine felt a hand on her back, "Look Raine, you're my baby sister and no matter what, I love you. I love you more than you could ever know. Let me go with you when you meet Damien. If I like what he says, I'll back you to the hilt."

Raine looked up at Penny, "Really? You would back me if you like what he says?

Penny shook her head, "Yes. I'll back you up."

Raine asked, "Will you go in with an open heart and mind?"

"Yes, I will go in with an open heart and an open mind. At the end of the day, you are my baby sister and I can't let you make this decision alone. I will be there for you now and forever."

Raine laid her head on her big sister's shoulder, "Thanks Penny. I love you too big sis."

The two ladies stood up and embraced each other. Raine felt good that her sister decided to at least hear Damien out. Since their mother's passing the two of them had not gotten along well; but this moment, was how she remembered her relationship with her sister being before they loss their mother.

Since Raine was a child, her big sister was always there for her. She would pick Raine up from school and walk her home. Sometimes, they would go by the local playground and swing on the swings. Raine loved those days. Penny was her idol for so long. The five years difference in age was nothing to them.

Nya on the other hand, wasn't as close to Raine. Nya's subconscious resentment of Raine made them fight all the time. The strange thing about their relationship is that no one else could do any harm to Raine or they would have to answer to Nya.

The two ladies walked into the living room where their father was watching television. They stood on each side of his chair and Penny spoke, "Daddy, I'm going to go with Raine and talk to this guy. Please be understanding and don't hate her."

Cornelius stood up and put his arms around Raine, "Baby girl, I could never hate you. I don't like what you are trying to do, but you are my daughter and I won't hate my own child."

He turned to his oldest daughter, "Penny, I know you are wise for your 27 years. Don't let them drag you and my baby girl down."

Penny hugged her daddy, "I won't Daddy; I'll listen to what he has to say. We promise we won't make a decision until we come back here and talk to you, okay?"

Raine chimed in, "Yeah Daddy, we won't make a decision until we come back and talk to you."

Cornelius looked at Penny then Raine. He spoke softly, "A year ago I lost the most important woman in my life. I don't want to lose my daughters too."

Nya walked up behind them, "I'm not going anywhere, Daddy. I'm standing firm with God and you."

Raine looked coldly at Nya. She knew that was a play to be daddy's girl. They didn't need that at this moment. She decided not to address it.

Cornelius motioned to Nya, "Come over here baby."

They all embraced one another. Raine loved this moment. It hadn't happened in a long time. Even with the anger she felt towards Nya, she still loved moments like this one. Deep inside, she hoped it would never end.

Chapter 3

Damien sat in his office with his friend, Don. Damien and Don had worked together for the last ten years, recruiting and training talent for Fresh City Records.

Damien said, "Man, I finally met those two sisters today and they are fine, you hear me?" One is about twenty-seven and other one is about twenty-two. Both can sing, but that twenty-two year old is hot; I want that."

Don smiled, "Yeah can she sing or are you just trying to hit it?"

"Man, both. Boy she got a butt on her! I watched her go to her car and couldn't take my eyes off of it, you know what I mean. I had some visions going boy. I haven't heard her sing but I may give her a contract just to get with her."

Don threw his head back and laughed, "You stupid. What about the other one?"

"I don't know man. She can sing but she seems to be stuck on her beliefs. I don't know if we need a devout Christian 'round here messing things up. She might get in the heads of some of my other talent and convince them to leave. We need more devils here, not Saints."

Don nodded, "But as long as you got a contract on them, they ain't going nowhere; you know what I mean?"

"True dat, but we still don't need her around here. I want to hear that young girl sing. If she's good, she's getting a deal."

Don asked, "What about Elaine?"

Damien sighed, "What about her? I'm tired of her. Man, she's getting on my nerves. You know I can't go anywhere without her asking me where I'm going, what I'm doing, blah, blah, blah. You know?"

"Yeah."

Damien continued, "I'm 30 years old and my momma don't ask me where I'm going. Finally, last night I had to pull off my belt and teach her a lesson. I had to teach her not to be messing in my business."

Don put his hand over his mouth, "Ohhhh, no wonder I haven't seen her around here today. She isn't going to call the police is she?"

Damien laughed, "She better not. She knows where her smack comes from."

Don said, "Yeah. You're an artist at stringing them out man."

Damien laughed, "Yeah you just gotta know what to do my brother. Get them hooked, then you can do whatever you want to them and they won't leave. But if I get this fine sweet thing, I'll be kicking Elaine out. She's made me enough money anyway and the suits don't care about her anymore either."

Don smiled, "Yeah, she was good but she just ain't great you know? That's what we need is a great singer to put us on the map. I hope your girl is the one."

Damien nodded, "I hope so too. If she can sing as good as her sister we'll be in business for a long time."

"The sister was that good?"

"Boy, you just don't know. That girl can blow. I felt a chill up and down my spine when she was singing and you know I don't know nobody's Jesus. She had me 'bout to run up to the altar. Ya feel me?"

Don reared back laughing, "Dang, then she must've been tearing it up my brother."

"You know, she was killing it. Then when I talked to her about a deal, all she wanted to know was if she was going to be singing gospel. Man, ain't no money in gospel; what the heck she talking about?"

"I know that pissed you off," said Don.

"Heck yeah, I was mad as could be. I came out there, sat through that church service and for what...just to hear this girl talk about singing gospel. I wanna get rich and gospel won't get me there."

Don agreed, "I know that's right. Well maybe her sister will be just as good without the Jesus stuff."

Damien nodded, "Yeah, I think so brother. She looked like she would have been down to sign right now. My boy Derrick said she's better than the girl I heard today. If that's true we'll be rich boy."

Don rubbed his hands together, "So when she coming?"

Damien answered, "Tomorrow evening. I'm meeting her at LaRusso's on 50th. I'll feed her and then bring her back here to hear what she got. Hopefully, if she's good, I can sign her tomorrow night."

"And knock it out too?" said Don.

"Hey that would be a bonus whether she can sing or not. You know."

They both laughed and continued to talk for another hour. Afterwards, Damien went back to his apartment. He unlocked the door and went inside.

***

Elaine was the star of Fresh City Records and Damien's current girlfriend. He discovered her two years before and signed her to a contract. However, she never rose to the level that he believed she could have.

Now, he was disgusted with her. She was strung out on drugs and he beat her regularly. Her second CD didn't make the top 50 on the charts and Damien blamed her for it. He wanted to kick her out but he didn't have any new talent to replace her with.

Elaine sat on the couch with her friend Daphne. Daphne despised Damien. Damien hated the type of woman Daphne was because she was a fighter. Elaine was submissive and would take a beating just to stay with Damien. Daphne would fight Damien to the bitter end. She came up in the streets and didn't take smack from anyone.

Daphne waved her hands in the air, "You're a coward and a punk. Why don't you fight me?"

Damien turned away, "You better get away from me woman."

Daphne continued, "Yeah that's what I thought, punk."

Elaine stood up and grabbed Daphne's hand, "Come on girl, its okay. I'll be alright. It was my fault."

Daphne stomped her foot, "No it wasn't! No woman deserves this kind of treatment."

Elaine said, "Just let it go Daphne, please."

Damien walked into the bedroom hardly paying them any attention. He knew if Raine was talented at all, Elaine would be gone the next day. He wasn't concerned about Daphne.

When he was in the bedroom his cell phone rang. He didn't recognize the number, "Hello, Damien Black of Fresh City Records."

The voice said, "Hi, This is Penny Davis from church."

Damien smiled, "Well, I didn't expect to hear from you. What can I do for you?"

Penny answered, "Tomorrow I will be coming with my sister Raine. I'll have an open mind as to what you say but my sister is my heart and I'm not going to let you near her without me; are we clear?"

Damien was angry. How dare this church going woman talk to him like that. He knew he had to be polite to have a chance to sign either of them, "As a crystal ball, Miss Davis."

Penny noted the sarcasm, "We'll see you tomorrow; good night."

Damien frowned, "Good night." He hung up the phone and cursed. He didn't like Penny even more now. She reminded him of Daphne.

He settled into his bed and decided to go to sleep. Tomorrow he would map out his strategy for recruiting Raine Davis.

Chapter 4

Raine was in her bedroom getting ready for dinner and her audition at the studio. She had never been this excited before in her life. She only hoped that her sister would not ruin it for her.

She remembered what her mom would say every time she thought she would go off to California. She knew if her mother was looking down on her that she would not approve. But Raine believed she was destined to be a star and she was going to pursue her dream.

She decided to wear her purple blouse and black skirt. Her friends told her the purple blouse matched her skin-color beautifully and she wanted to make a good impression on Damien. She put on her favorite bracelet and took a good look at herself in the mirror. There was a knock at her door; she answered, "Who is it?"

"It's your Dad, baby girl."

"Come on in, Daddy."

Her Dad entered the room with a smile on his face. She was happy to see that smile and hoped she could keep it there. She wanted this contract more than anything but she knew the price might be her father's disapproval.

"No matter how much I might disapprove of what you're doing, I do believe that you are a great singer. You will do so well that they will have no choice but to sign you. All I ask is that you please don't forget the God you serve," said Cornelius.

"I won't forget Daddy, I promise. I'm so glad that you're smiling right now. You don't know what that means to me."

He hugged her and she was happier than ever. This was a sign to her and it was her time. It was her time to rise up to the top of the world and her daddy's approval was all the confirmation she needed.

He turned and left the room. She stood there watching him until he was gone. She looked in the mirror again and touched up her makeup and hair. She was ready. She felt she could conquer the world.

Raine walked into the living room. Penny and Cornelius were talking when she walked in the room. Raine walked up to Penny and hugged her. She didn't want there to be any issues between them on her big audition.

Penny said, "Raine, you do know that Fresh City Records is not a major player in the music world right? This Damien guy may not be able to deliver what he's saying."

Raine nodded, "I do, but that won't stop me from becoming a star. I just need somewhere to start and get noticed."

Penny stared at her, "I did some research on Damien. He doesn't have a great reputation."

"I thought you said you were going to have an open mind about all of this?"

"Raine, I do have an open mind," said Penny, " but you have to research these people. The news reports believe he's beating his girlfriend."

"What does that have to do with me? I'm not his girlfriend; I'm trying to start my singing career."

Penny continued, "It just means that he's a man of questionable character and you have to be careful with him. Maybe we should talk to his girlfriend, Elaine."

"Why?" Raine rolled her eyes, "Who is she and what can she say?"

"You know Elaine," said Penny, "She made that song, 'My Man Don't Cheat', a couple of years ago; that's his girlfriend."

Raine perked up, "Yeah, I remember that song. If I had sung it, it would have been a hit. Just because she didn't make it doesn't mean I won't."

Penny looked at her father, "Okay Raine. Let's go see what he's got to say."

Raine looked down and sighed, "Okay. Let's go."

Raine hugged her father one more time and headed out the door. The two ladies got in their car and headed to the restaurant for dinner.

***

The sisters arrive at LaRusso's a few minutes after seven. They barely spoke to each other in the car. Raine sensed that Penny would try and derail her audition and she wasn't going to stand for it. This was her once in a lifetime opportunity. She thought, *'How many AR's show up at your door? This is the biggest chance I got and she's not about to mess it up for me.'*

Damien stood at the entrance waiting. He reached out to Raine and gave her a hug, "Thank you for coming out this evening baby." He turned to Penny and hugged her, "Hi Penny."

Penny gave a dry hug, "Good evening."

Damien motioned, "Allow me." He led them through the front door and to a table in the restaurant."

Raine asked, "Oh you got a table already."

Damien answered, "I have a standing reservation here and several other places. Fresh City Records is big in this town and most establishments will give us a reservation when they won't give it to others. We got it like that. When you become a part of the team, you'll get the same respect and admiration in this town and all over the country."

Raine showed all of her thirty-two teeth, "Sounds great to me." She looked at Penny and realized she wasn't impressed. Raine grew angry inside. She felt her sister was there just to mess things up for her.

Penny asked, "Where's your girlfriend?"

The question made Raine cringed. This was not what she wanted Penny there to do. If she ruined her opportunity she would never speak to her again.

Damien answered the question, "She's not feeling well. I usually invite her to these recruiting dinners, but she's ill."

Penny nodded her head, "Too bad. I would have loved to talk to her and get her take on things."

Damien appeared to be annoyed with the remark. Raine jumped in hoping to calm things down, "So, I'll get to audition in a real studio?"

"Of course," said Damien, "We have a state of the art studio with the finest engineers you will ever be associated with. But what we need is talent. I thought

Elaine was going to put us on the map but she's not working out. I may have to let her go."

Raine said, "Wow, really? I thought she was good but why can't she sell any records."

Damien looked at Penny and then back at Raine. Before he could answer, the waiter came to the table. Raine was not going to let it go, she wanted to know the answer to the question. After the waiter left the table she asked again, "What happened to Elaine, why couldn't she sell any records?"

Damien sighed, "Well, I'll be honest. When we first recruited Elaine she had all the talent in the world. Her first single rose to number 8 on the charts. I saw nothing but success in her future. However, she got herself mixed up with drugs. By the time I found out, she was deeply addicted. I tried to get help for her but she would just have one of her junkie friends sneak drugs in the rehab facility."

"I don't see that problem with you. You come from a strong Christian family with a good foundation. I don't think you will fall prey to drugs. The ones who don't, end up a success."

Penny said, "Are you going to seriously sit there and pretend you didn't know she was using, come on really?"

Damien sighed again, "Look Penny, I'm on the road a lot looking for new talent. On one stretch I was gone for about four months. During that time, her so called friends got her hooked on cocaine. When I returned, I found the drugs but it was too late, she was already hooked. Then, like I said, I've tried to get her help but she has to want it. Now, all she wants to do is sit around and get high. I need someone willing to work long hours making music and selling records, not a junkie."

Raine said, "I can see where he wouldn't have known Penny. Just let it go, okay." She was pleading with her sister not to ruin this for her but Penny just wouldn't let it go. She kept asking questions and making comments.

The waiter returned with their drinks and to take their order. Raine was happy for the distraction. After they ordered she said she needed to go to the ladies room. She hoped her sister would join her, so they could talk.

Raine excused herself and Penny decided to join her. In the ladies room Raine turned and put her hand on her hip, "You're going to ruin this for me. Why don't you shut your mouth and have an open mind like you said you would or was that a lie or something just to get down here and screw this up for me? You make me sick sometimes and I wish you had never come with me."

Penny listened with her arms crossed, "Raine I'm trying to protect..."

Raine interjected, "You're not trying to do anything, except ruin this for me. You're just jealous and you can't stand the fact that I'm going to be a star and you're going to be stuck singing in a local choir the rest of your life."

Penny replied, "Raine, that's not true."

"It is true. You're mad because you're a washed up has been at twenty-seven and I'm going to be a bigger star than any of you. Heck, you're still singing old songs in church. Everybody is wondering why you can't move on. I think it's because you just lost your talent."

Raine knew her comments would hurt and she wanted to take it back but didn't.

Penny stared for a minute, "Okay Raine. Do what you please. This washed up has been will leave you to make whatever choices you want. Don't call me when it all caves in on you!"

Raine watched her sister storm out, "I won't." Part of her wanted to stop her but part of her was glad she was gone.

She looked in the mirror and reasoned that she looked great and her two sisters were jealous of her. She didn't care. She was going to be a star and that's all that mattered.

Chapter 5

Penny came back to the table while Raine remained in the ladies room. Damien sat there with a smug look on his face. She stopped and looked Damien in the eye, "My sister may be blinded by you, but I'm not. If anything happens to her, I will be coming after you."

Damien stood up and motioned to a man who was about to come over. He said, "Why would I want anything to happen to your sister? If she can sing anywhere near what I heard from you, she will make me tons of money. It's in my best interest that nothing happens to Raine."

Penny only met this man the day before but she knew she couldn't stand him. The smug look on his face made her cringe deep inside her gut. She wanted to slap him but she knew that wouldn't be lady-like or Christian. She decided to just walk out of the restaurant.

As she turned to leave, she saw Raine coming back to the table. Penny just stared at her as she walked out. Raine stopped. It made Penny think she wanted to say something else but Penny didn't want to hear it. She was hurt by the comments her little sister said to her in the ladies room. She walked swiftly toward the exit.

Raine said things in the past but never was she that hurtful with her comments. She had lost it and Penny knew it. Penny knew Raine was headed for disaster but she couldn't stop it.

The look she saw in Raine's eyes told her that Raine was prepared to do anything to make it. On the way to the car she started to cry but managed to hold back the tears. She wanted to hate her sister for what she said but she couldn't. She loved her and she knew if Raine needed her she would be there in a flash.

Penny got in the car, dropped her head on the steering wheel and prayed, *"Father, this evening has not turned out as I would have liked it to. My baby sister is in there with a man that I believe does not have her best interest at heart. Lord, I ask that you protect my sister. Help her in this situation. Help her to see the bad in this man. Help her to see that he doesn't have her best interest in mind. There's nothing that I can do as a woman but you God can do anything. In your matchless son Jesus' name I pray...Amen."*

Penny headed home trying to figure out how she was going to tell her father what happened. Her father was relying on her to stop Raine from signing but instead she all but delivered her sister right into the hands of this man she knew wasn't right.

Raine was headstrong and believed she knew what was best for her. She was solely focused on making it and nothing else mattered. Penny wished her mom was there because her mom could control Raine.

Since their mother's death Raine respected her father but she became more and more out of control with each passing day. She did what she wanted when she wanted because all she had to do was bat her eyes or start to cry and their dad would forgive her. Their mom would never have fallen for the things that Raine was doing.

One day a few months ago, Penny caught Raine smoking marijuana. This devastated Penny and her father. All Raine did was cry and say she was missing her mom so much and couldn't help it. A few minutes later Penny overheard Raine telling her boyfriend what happened. Raine laughed at how she had fooled all of them.

Penny thought the best thing she could do was to call Raine's boyfriend, Jay. Maybe he could have some impact on pulling Raine back from the clutches of Damien Black.

Chapter 6

Raine sat down at the table across from Damien and slowly and seductively crossed her legs. She smiled inside but on the outside she tried to maintain her cool. Now she knew everything was in her lap. She controlled her own destiny and she didn't have to worry about her sister messing anything up.

The look on Damien's face said it all. She had his complete attention. She showed her pearly whites, trying to attract him even more. She knew she could sing so that wasn't the issue. She wanted him to like, or even love her but most of all she wanted him to sign her to a deal.

Damien sipped his drink, "Is everything okay?"

Raine shuffled in her seat, "Yes, everything is fine…now."

Damien inched up to the table with a smile like a Cheshire cat, "Well I can't say that I'm sorry to see your sister go. She was seriously ruining the mood."

"That…she was!" said Raine. "She was getting on my nerves. They're all jealous of me because I'm the prettiest and most talented in the family. I also have the drive and initiative to go to the next level while all they want to do is stay here and waste away. I don't want to be twenty-seven and still singing in church, you know?"

Damien smiled, "Really. You are the prettiest and that's for sure…the finest too. I can't wait to see that talent."

Raine asked, "Well, you will in the studio hun."

Damien reared back with confidence, "So, you have a boyfriend?"

The question surprised Raine. She wasn't sure how to answer it. If she said 'yes' would that hurt her chances? She decided to be honest, "Yes I do but what does that matter. I mean, you have Elaine right?"

Damien shrugged it off, "I broke up with her last night. I can't handle all the drama anymore. You know what I mean?"

Raine was confused, "I thought you said she didn't come because she was sick?"

Damien replied, "I did…to your nosey sister. The truth is I broke up with her because it was too much drama with the drugs and alcohol."

Raine's forehead wrinkled, "Was it that bad?"

"If only you knew," said Damien. "So I can honestly say, I'm in the market and you have captivated my heart."

Raine was shocked. She didn't know how to respond to that statement. Now she found herself wishing Penny hadn't left her alone with him. No wonder he was touching her so much the day before. He liked her and wanted more than to sign her, he wanted her to be his girlfriend.

She laughed it off, "Well as I said, I have a boyfriend, so I'm not on the market. Anyway you just met me yesterday."

Damien shrugged his shoulders, "Doesn't mean I can't be captivated by what I have seen so far. Do you love him?"

Raine scooted away from him, "Damien, what does that have to do with my singing? Yes, I love him."

Damien continued, "I'm just trying to see if there's an opening baby. You might have a boyfriend but you might be thinking of trading him in for someone new. But you're right; it has nothing to do with music, so let's talk music."

Raine smiled trying not to make Damien mad at her and cause her to lose her opportunity, "Thank you."

"How long have you been singing?"

Raine laughed, "How long have I been alive? My mom use to say I was singing before I talked."

"Wow that's amazing. The great ones often have stories like that. What are you going to sing for me tonight?"

Raine thought carefully before she answered, "Well, I think I'm going to sing Whitney Houston's, 'I'll Always Love You'. That's one of my all-time favorite songs."

Damien nodded, "I love that song too. Are you going to sing it as good as Whitney?"

"Whitney's one of my idols and I only hope I can do it as well as she does. All my friends and family say I do it just as well if not better so I guess it will depend on you."

Damien nodded, "Yeah, I guess it will but anyway if you're as good as your sister then I know we'll be making big dollars. I got some songs just waiting for the right talent."

Raine grew with excitement but she had to be careful. Damien made it clear that he wanted her but she didn't want to cross a line with him. After all she had Jay and she loved him so much. She didn't realize that before but now she did.

Chapter 7

Raine was so happy inside that she could hardly contain herself. She was sitting in the booth at Fresh City Records studios waiting to audition for Damien. If she could impress Damien then he would give her an opportunity to impress his bosses.

Raine was thinking, *'This is my chance, my opportunity. I will not let this blessing pass me by. I know I have what it takes, God has given me the gift and the passion to exceed and nothing, I mean nothing will stop me!'* She bent her arms and clinched her fist. *'I can do this, No! I will do this for God is my witness I can do all things through Him!'*

She could see Damien, two men and a woman in the engineer booth talking. Her anxiety heightened with each passing second. After a while, she heard Damien's voice over the speakers, "Okay sweetheart, you ready to show us what you got?"

Raine swallowed hard, "Oh yes."

She took a deep breath, *"If I should stay, well I would only be in your way. And so I'll go, and yet I know, that I'll think of you every step of the way..."*

Before Raine knew it, she was off and running singing better than she had ever sung before in her life. She blocked out everything and everyone around her and put her heart and mind into the song. She knew she was killing it better than Whitney Houston ever did.

She got to the chorus and gently hit the high notes as only she could. She didn't look in the booth because she didn't want to be distracted.

When she was done she was exhausted. She looked at the faces of the people in the booth and they were all smiling and nodding. She felt good inside and waited to hear what Damien had to say.

Damien came in the booth and stood in front of her. He paused for seemed like years to Raine, "That was the best I have ever heard that song in my life. Whitney couldn't have done it better."

Raine jumped up and down clapping. She was knocking at the door of her dream. She managed to say, "Really, I just blocked out everything and everybody and sung with all my heart."

Damien smiled and nodded his head, "Well baby it was great. Now I just have to get you in front of my boss. Once he hears you, I know you're in."

"Okay, so what do I do now?" said Raine.

"Well, just hold on for a minute and let me talk to these guys."

Raine was excited, "Okay." She watched as Damien went back and talked to the other people in the booth. They all shook hands and Damien came back in the booth where Raine waited.

"Well my boss will be here at about seven in the morning. My place is right across the street so how about we go there and chill until he comes in?"

Raine didn't want to hear that, "Damien I can't do that. I need to go home. I can come back in the morning but I can't stay with you overnight."

Damien said, "Look baby, this is a moving business. Things happen quickly. If you go home and my boss comes in early and leaves then I don't know when I'll be able to get you in front of him. My place is right across the street so as soon as he comes in we can shoot over here and you can sing for him. But it's your choice, I'll take you home and you can take your chances if you like. I can't promise you anything if you leave now."

Raine didn't want to go to Damien's apartment. She may have done some wild things lately but something like this was out of her league. She had a boyfriend that she cared about. She wasn't completely sure that she loved him but she cared enough about him and what she believed in not to sleep with Damien.

She squirmed in her stance, "I don't...I don't think that's a...I...I can't Damien. There's got to be another way."

Damien frowned, "Okay, I'll take you home. You can come back in the morning and take your chances." He walked out of the booth and Raine followed. Fear of losing her dream consumed every inch of her being. In her mind she considered Damien's offer but the thought of Jay and what she felt for him stopped her from doing it. She believed that she could avoid anything Damien tried but what if he didn't stop? Now she truly regretted running Penny away.

She followed behind Damien as he headed for his limo to take her home. She considered changing her mind again. She thought about going to his place and that she wouldn't have to do anything. She could just wait there until the morning. All she could envision was Damien forcing her to have sex with him and she just couldn't.

Raine got in the limo and Damien instructed the driver to take her home. Raine asked, "You're not getting in?"

Damien didn't reply. He just slammed the door and the limo drove off. Raine feared that her opportunity was gone. She began to cry. The tears started slowly but then streamed down her face endlessly. She thought, *'I was so close. All I had to do was stay with him for one night and I could have had my dream. Why did I have to be raised with morals? I hate being a Christian.'*

The limo pulled up in front of Raine's house. She saw her boyfriend's car sitting out front. She knew Penny called him to tell him what she was trying to do. She stayed in the limo to clean her face up.

She got out the limo and went inside the house where she saw Jay sitting in the living room alone. He stood up slowly as she walked in the door. Raine didn't know what to say to him. She hadn't done anything wrong but she certainly considered it. In her mind, that was wrong enough. She tried to look him in the eyes, but couldn't.

Raine stood there for a second hoping Jay would talk first. He didn't.

"Hi baby," she said. She shifted her weight from side to side, "What are you doing here?"

"You know why I'm here. Why didn't you tell me you were going to audition for Fresh City Records?"

Raine squirmed, "Because I wanted to surprise you if I got a contract. Wouldn't that be great? We could be on our way to success."

Jay nodded his head with a smirk on his face, "That's funny Raine. I considered us a success already. I'll graduate with honors in June and you're doing great in college. I already have a job lined up with Corinthians

Technology making very good money. What you consider success is different than what I consider success."

"But I wanna sing. Why is that so wrong?"

Jay walked over and put his hands on Raine's shoulders, "It's not wrong to sing. What's wrong is singing for people like Damien Black and Fresh City Records. He doesn't mean well for you."

"How do you know that Jay?" said Raine. "All I did tonight was have dinner and audition at the studio. Then he brought me home. Nothing happened. God, y'all always assume the worst." She tried to walk off but Jay grabbed her and held her closely.

She felt something she hadn't in a long while and she knew it was love. This man who she had been dating for six years loved her and truly cared for her. He had been there for the best of times and the worst of times. She was so glad she didn't go to Damien's place but she regretted even thinking about going.

Jay said, "Nothing happened tonight but what about tomorrow, or the next day? That contract will have a high price to pay."

She put her arms tightly around her man, "Jay, I love you and I would never cross you." She wanted him to feel the love she had for him; love she herself didn't know she had at that very moment. It took Damien to threaten that existence to make her realize that the love she felt for Jay was real.

They hugged tightly. Raine felt like she was in Heaven. She liked feeling this way about Jay. It had been awhile since she could honestly say she loved him. But at this moment in time, she did know that she loved him.

"Can you come home with me," said Jay?

Raine smiled. She knew what that meant and she wanted it. She cried earlier because she believed she might have loss her dream but now she was happy she didn't go with Damien. She was going to her boyfriend's house to make love to him. He was the only man she had made love to in her whole life.

"I have to go back to the studio at seven, so I'll need to drive my car," she said. " I'll gather some of my clothes and meet you at your place in a few minutes."

Jay smiled, "Okay, I'll be there waiting for you." He leaned down and kissed her and her emotions overflowed. The kiss only confirmed that she actually loved him.

Chapter 8

Raine's alarm on her phone sounded throughout the room, waking her and Jay up from their sleep. She wanted to get up early and be at the studio before seven. She kissed Jay as he lay on the bed and ran into the bathroom to get ready.

She was filled with enthusiasm. She sang all her favorite songs as she got dressed. When she came out of the bathroom Jay was sitting up in the bed.

"Don't go," said Jay. She stopped in her tracks. That was the last thing she needed to hear and frankly she was becoming irritated with the naysayers she was surrounded by. No one wanted her to get the contract so she started believing all of them were against her success. Jay continued, "Stay here and continued what we started."

Raine smiled. Now that offer was tempting and better than anything Penny said. She enjoyed every moment of the night before and wouldn't mind a little bit more but this was her dream and she had to pursue it. She was renewed in her belief that she could make it happen and not sacrifice what she believed in. She believed that Damien would leave her alone now that he saw where she stood.

She replied, "Jay, baby, I have to go for this. My dream is right in front of me baby. If I don't see this through I will always wonder what I could've been. If I don't get a contract, then I promise, I'll just leave it alone; but think about it, how often do AR men come around and this one landed right at my church like it was ordained or something."

"What if he requires you to do more than sing?"

"Why do all of you think that? Oh my God I'm sick of hearing it. Come on baby, that won't be the case. They all loved my singing and all I have to do now is sing for the big man and I'm in the door. I can be the next Whitney baby. Wouldn't you be happy for me?"

Jay smirked, "Yes baby, I would be happy for you. The thing is I would be happy for you if you flipped burgers at McDonalds. I just want you to be in my life, forever."

"Then why don't you come with me," she said?

"I can't. Remember I have to travel. We have a game tonight."

"Oh, I did forget. How far do you have to travel?"

"We have to go to Georgia. I probably won't be back until the early morning. Maybe we can hook up and spend the day tomorrow?"

Raine poked him in the chest, "Count on it baby. I gotta run sweetie."

"Okay honey, be safe. Please be safe."

They kissed. Raine didn't want to let go but she knew she had to get to that studio before Damien's boss got there.

***

Raine got to Fresh City Records a few minutes before seven. The receptionist greeted her at the front. Raine said, "I'm supposed to meet Damien Black here this morning."

"One minute." She dialed the number and waited, "Hi Mr. Black, I have..." She motioned to Raine.

"Raine Davis."

"I have Raine Davis here to see you." She waited a minute while the receptionist listened to Damien, "Yes sir."

The receptionist gently hung up the phone and then whale-eyed Raine, "I'm sorry but he's busy right now." The receptionist looked away, "He said he'll give you a call tomorrow."

Raine's heart dropped. The receptionist confirmed her fear that she had loss her opportunity to become a star. She dropped her head and walked out the building.

She sat in her car crying when someone startled her by tapping on her window. It was Damien. He motioned for her to follow him. She quickly stepped out her car and followed Damien to his limo.

She got in after him and sat quietly while he said something to the driver. When he was finished he turned to her and said, "I told you that if you went home you could miss your opportunity, didn't I?"

Raine slowly nodded her head.

Damien continued, "My boss came in early…'bout six. He left 30 minutes later and won't be back until tomorrow, maybe. If you had been at my place we could have come over and handled this audition but now you've made me look bad to everyone. I don't think I can sign you now."

Raine eyes welled with tears, "Damien please, give me another chance. I'll camp out here in my car and wait for him, if that's what it takes."

"You should have done that last night. No, you should have come to my place like I asked you to do." He shook his head, "I don't think you have what it takes to make it in this business."

Raine inched up on her seat and put her hand on Damien's knee, "Please Damien give me one more chance." Raine realized just how desperate she was. Thoughts ran across her mind. Many of which she didn't think she would ever entertain.

Damien took her hand and pulled her to her knees and between his legs. He kissed her in the mouth and Raine surrendered to his moves. She wanted that audition and now she was about to allow herself to be used by Damien. It was against everything she believed in. She didn't like it at all but she didn't want to blow her chance to get a contract.

Damien reached behind Raine and down her backside. He grabbed her behind and squeezed it tightly, while looking in her eyes the entire time. Raine wanted to scream but she was too scared, too afraid to lose her dream. Damien said, "You want another chance don't you?"

Raine sobbed. She wanted another chance but she didn't want to pay the price for it.

Damien pushed her away, "Get out my limo and don't come back. You won't ever make it in this business."

"Okay, okay, Damien. I'll do it."

Damien turned his head to the side and shouted, "What, I didn't hear you?"

A little louder Raine said, "I'll do it."

He unzipped his pants and grabbed Raine's head. He forced it between his legs. Damien made Raine performed oral sex on him. She hated every minute of it. She closed her eyes and imagined she was somewhere, somewhere with Jay but the thought of Jay and what she was doing sickened her. She thought she could never face him again.

Damien pulled her clothes off and laid her on the limo seat. She didn't resist. She wanted it to be over quickly but Damien took his time and had sex with Raine. It was the first time she had sex with someone other than Jay.

Afterwards Damien put his clothes back on, like the sex meant nothing to him at all. He then made a phone call. Raine slowly got up and put her clothes on. She tried hard not to cry but the tears came out anyway. She blocked any thoughts of her family and Jay out of her mind. They were all right and she was wrong. She sold her body to get a contract. The sad thing she realized was that she wasn't even sure if Damien would keep his end up.

Damien said, "When you finish getting dressed come on in the studio. My boss is waiting to hear you sing."

Raine looked up sharply. She really started crying because Damien lied to her and she knew it. His boss was there the whole time.

Damien grabbed her by the arm, "You need to get it together if you want that contract. I need you to make me some money; you hear me?"

Raine opened her mouth wide, "You're hurting me."

Damien pulled her face close to his face, "I own you now. Get it together and sing this song like you never sung it before or you'll never be in the music business. You got it?"

Raine answered "Okay, okay."

Damien got out of the limo and left Raine crying. She realized that Penny and Jay were right. In order to get this contract she had to sell her soul. The worst part was that she did it. She wanted it so badly that she gave in and gave herself to Damien. She was ashamed and could never go back home.

***

Raine got herself together and now she was back in the one place where she felt the best. Standing in that studio booth ready to sing was her zone, her place where no one could harm her or force her to do anything against her morals. It was her world there and she was comfortable in it.

The engineering booth had more people in it. These people were different from the people who were in the booth the night before. These people wearing suits and sharp dresses, they seemed very important and even Damien was submissive to them. Almost as if he was afraid of them.

The engineer gave Raine her cue and she got into the moment. She blocked out the incident in the limo and got into her element. She sung like it was the only thing she was born to do. She just kept singing and singing, not paying any attention to the people in the booth, what happened to her in the limo or her family. She did what she was born to do, sing.

When it was over, no one cheered. No one said anything to her at all. She just stood in the booth waiting for something. Thoughts ran across her mind, *'Did she sacrifice her morals for nothing? Did Damien lie to her again and this was all a farce?'* She wanted to start crying but she held it inside.

Raine felt a cringe in her stomach. She was so nervous. After a few moments Damien came hurriedly into the booth, "They love you." He smiled and put his hands on her shoulders, "They really love you."

She hated the touch of his hands but the news was too great for her to be concerned. He did deliver his promise. She was getting her contract. Raine smiled, "Really?"

Damien answered, "Yes and they want to sign you to a contract…right now!"

Raine was excited, "Yippee! Oh my God, I can't believe this is happening for me." She completely forgot about the incident in the limo.

Damien looked at the room where the people stood, "Raine, I have to tell you something. These people, they are not to be played with. Once you sign this contract, it's for life. You understand?"

Raine's forehead wrinkled, "Life? I will have a record deal for the rest of my life?"

Damien licked his lips, "Yeah, but listen. They will make you a star. That's guaranteed but you can never leave them. They see everything you do and everything you say. They're clients consist of people like Michael Jackson and Whitney Houston."

Raine said, "Michael Jackson and Whitney Houston? They aren't on the same label."

Damien said, "True, but they both worked for these people."

Raine shifted her weight, "You're scaring me."

"Look, don't be scared. Just know that you are about to make more money than you will ever be able to spend and you will be more famous than you could ever imagine. But most of all remember you can't quit...ever!"

Raine smiled, "Why would I want to quit; that's the life I've been wanting."

Damien put his arm around her, "Good, then let's do this contract."

Raine asked, "Don't I need a lawyer or something?"

Damien replied, "Like I told you yesterday, if you wait you won't get a contract. You can go get a lawyer but these people...these people won't wait for you. They will move on to the next person. What do you want to do?"

Raine thought for a second. She couldn't let this opportunity pass her by. She had lost her morals for the sake of this chance so she wasn't going to screw it up now.

"Okay, let's do this now. More money than I can spend?"

Damien smiled, "More money than both of us can spend."

Raine looked in the booth; everyone except the engineers was gone. She followed Damien down a corridor and into a dimly lit room far away from all the recording booths and offices. That feeling in the pit of her stomach was coming back, "Damien this room is scary."

Damien replied, "Don't worry baby, it's alright. I've been in here before."

Damien stopped at a table and Raine stood by him. Across from the table was a man but Raine couldn't make out his face. The room was too dim for her to see him.

The man asked, "Did you explain the rule to her Damien?"

Damien answered, "Yes, I did and she's on board."

The man said, "Good." He slid a piece of paper across the table and in front of Raine, "Are you prepared to sign this music contract with us?"

Raine answered, "Yes."

"Then sign it," he said.

Raine replied, "I need a pen." Another man came from around the table and Damien took Raine by the shoulders and held her tightly. Raine tried to wiggle out from Damien's grip, but to no avail. The man pulled out a knife and Raine shouted, "What are you doing?"

The man took Raine's hand and held it open. He cut a slit down the palm of her hand. Raine screamed from the pain. The man took her hand pushed it down on the paper.

The first man said, "We do not use pens, we sign in blood."

Raine watched as the man whose face she couldn't see slit the palm of his hand and pressed it down on the paper. He said, "Now, we have a deal."

***

Raine sat in Damien's office while he talked on the phone. He made calls about her to advance her career. It was happening so fast Raine couldn't believe it. Her hand was wrapped in bandages but she could still feel the pain.

Damien finished his call and walked over to the couch. He sat next to Raine, "Hey baby, things are moving fast for you. I have several songs for you to learn and we can start working on your first CD right away. Are you happy?"

Raine looked at him with her big eyes, "I am, but I'm a little scared too. Who signs a contract in blood?"

Damien tried to comfort her, "Look, don't worry about any of that. We're about to be rich beyond belief."

Raine said, "I want to go tell my family."

Damien answered, "You can't go home now. We're your family now Raine. If you go home they will try and convince you to stay with them. Plus we have tons of work to do."

Raine pleaded, "But I just can't leave my family. I told Jay I would come back and we would spend the day together tomorrow."

"Those days are over Raine. You need to be here in the studio working on your songs. That's the price you pay for success. It's all about the grind. If I were you, I would forget about your family and Jay. Besides I would make a better man for you anyway. Need I remind you of what we did? You don't love him and I know it."

Raine's head dropped, "But I do love him." In the back of her mind she realized that she couldn't look Jay in the eyes anymore after what she did in the limo. She was using her family and Jay as an excuse to get away for a few minutes to think and breathe. Too much was happening to fast.

"If you loved him so much then why did you make love to me? Don't make me regret signing on the first day."

Raine dropped her head again. She did love Jay but she was grateful that Damien kept his word and got her the contract. She had no love for him especially after what he did to her in the limo.

Damien walked over to the window, "Look, if you want to go back home for a night you can. But when you come back in the morning you belong to Fresh City Records. We have hours and hours of work to do and your family will only hinder that, understand?"

She stood up and gathered her purse, "Yes, I understand."

Damien put his arms around her and passionately kissed her in the mouth.

He said, "I'm your man now; don't forget that."

Out of fear, Raine laid her head on his chest, "Okay."

She turned and walked out of the office. She practically ran to her car and headed home. She didn't know what she was going to say to her family or most importantly, Jay. She did know two things though; she was not going to tell them about the limo and she was not going to tell them about signing in blood.

Chapter 9

Raine got home and was thankful no one was at the house. She wanted to shower and clean herself up as quickly as she could. Her hand felt better.

She ran into the house and headed straight for the shower. When she got in her room she peeled off her clothes piece by piece, leaving them on the floor as she walked closer to the shower.

She jumped in the shower and stayed under the water for what seemed like hours. Her hand felt so good that she ripped the bandages off and was stunned when she didn't see a scar. It was as if her hand was never cut.

There were some strange events happening to Raine but one thing was for sure. She was getting ready to be the big star she always imagined she would be. She could see herself on a big stage singing in front of all her family and friends. She paid a price but now it was time for success to come her way. She would get to throw it in Penny's face and she couldn't wait for that day to come.

She overheard Damien making plans for her to sing in the prestigious Peachtree Club. Only the city's best talent performed at that club and now she was going to have an opportunity to be the next one.

Raine finally got out of the shower and laid her naked body across her bed. She felt better about herself.

She still didn't know how or what she would tell her family but at least the stench of Damien was gone from her body.

She covered herself with her favorite blanket and before she knew it, she drifted off to sleep.

***

Raine was on stage singing; suddenly, the audience turned into demons. They began coming after her from all directions. She tried to run but she couldn't escape them. She ran and ran, falling along the way. She ran until she couldn't run anymore. Suddenly, they all were around her, ready to pounce on her. She didn't know what to do.

A loud bump suddenly woke Raine up from her dream. She was terrified by the nightmare and didn't know what to make of it. It seemed so real to her but she decided to blow it off and go see what the noise was in the other room.

She jumped up and put on some clothes. She found her father sitting in his favorite chair eating a sandwich. Cornelius said, "Raine, my baby, how are you? You didn't come home last night."

"I'm okay, Daddy; I stayed with Jay last night." She looked down knowing that father would not approve but she was ashamed of something far more treacherous than staying with Jay all night. She couldn't tell him what she had done to get an opportunity for a music contract and she certainly couldn't tell him about signing in blood.

"Sweetie, I can tell something is bothering you. You can't fool your dad; what is it?"

"Daddy, I signed a music contract with Fresh City Records today. I know you won't approve but I promise I will keep God first in everything I do; I promise."

Raine could see the disappointment in her father's eyes. He let go of his baby girl and eased back down in his favorite chair. The last thing Raine ever wanted to do was to hurt her father. So many things were going against the way she believed and now she hurt the one man who always loved her, no matter what.

Raine asked, "Daddy, are you okay?"

"I'm fine baby; I wish you all the success in the world." He never looked at Raine.

Raine knelt down in front of her dad. She looked him square in the face. He tried not to look at her but she took her hand to his chin and gently turned his face to hers, "Daddy, I will always love you no matter what. I know you don't approve of this but you will see that I'll be fine. I will be on top of the world. I will never turn away from you, my family or God."

Cornelius looked her deep in her eyes, "I have seen this before sweetheart and it doesn't end well for you, me or your sisters, especially Penny."

Raine was shocked, "Daddy, what are you talking about?"

Cornelius continued, "God has spoken to my heart and showed me the pain you will go through. It will not end well for anyone."

Raine deeply sighed and dropped her head, "Why is it that whenever I want to do something against the family's wishes, God always speaks to you or someone else; mom use to say the same thing. Why can't he be speaking to me? It's already done Daddy and I'm going to be a star and I'm going to buy you a big new house and a fancy car."

Cornelius nodded, "No baby. Keep those things. I don't want anything to do with any of that money."

Raine got angry. After all she endured; this man would turn down her gifts. She couldn't believe it, "Daddy, why would not take my money. I am going to earn it. I'm going to sell millions of records. It will be honest money."

"It may seem honest to you baby but it's not. It's the devil's money and I don't want any part of it."

Raine stood up, "Fine. I'll keep my money, my fame and everything else. My ungrateful family can stay right where they are…broke. Damien was right; I should have stayed at the studio."

Raine stomped off towards the kitchen. She heard her father say, "Lord help my baby girl." Raine nodded her head, "Oh my God."

While in the kitchen she decided to go to Jay's place. She had a key to his apartment. She was going to wait there for him to come back from his game. In the meantime she would figure out what to say to him. As she started to walk out, Nya came into the kitchen.

Nya looked at her little sister. Her stare was distant, like she didn't want to see her at all. She sat a bag of groceries and her purse on the table. She put her hand on her hip, "Well, you signed your deal huh; daddy's little girl has finally broke his heart? I can't say I didn't see that coming."

Raine and Nya often went at it. Since the passing of their mother it increased. They argued over everything. This was not going to be any different.

Raine folded her arms, "There you go, hatin' as usual. You just can't stand the fact that I'm going to be star and you'll still be here stuck in this house, as usual, doing nothing." Raine laughed and poked her finger at Nya.

"See you don't know anything. I want to be in this house, taking care of our father. You don't even notice how depressed and withdrawn he has been since momma died. You probably don't even care but everything must center around you. You have to be the center of attention all the time. So go on and be the star you want to be. Be the center of attention to the world. But here, you're just a self-centered little brat."

Raine snickered, "Yeah, well the world has to be centered on me because it can't be centered on you. I have more talent in my pinky finger than you do all together. Excuse me while I get out of this dump."

"Dump…this dump use to be your home." Nya rolled her eyes, "You use to love it and love us. Now you can't stand the sight of us because we're standing on our beliefs. Let me ask you, did singing get you that deal or did you spread your legs?"

Raine stood there looking at her for a minute wondering if she knew what happened in the limo. She reasoned that Nya was just assuming but she decided not to answer her question. Instead, she turned and exited. As she headed for the front door she shouted, "Bye, Daddy."

Cornelius didn't respond. Raine couldn't remember her father not responding to her or anyone else. She paused for a second hoping he would respond, but he never did. She looked down, ashamed, wondering if this was the last time she would see any of them. Then she walked out the door and to her car.

Chapter 10

Penny and her boyfriend Jaden came into the house. Her father was still sitting in his favorite chair. Penny could see the sadness written on his face, "Daddy." He didn't respond.

She called again, "Daddy, are you okay?"

Nya came in the room, "Raine finally finished breaking his heart. He hasn't moved in two hours."

Penny sighed, "She signed the contract didn't she?"

"Yep, you thought she wouldn't?" said Nya.

Penny nodded her head.

Nya continued, "You know there's no love lost between me and Raine. We haven't gotten along in years but even I'm afraid for her. She doesn't understand what's happening to her. She called this house a dump. As bad as Raine has been she's never been like that. The girl is changing already."

Penny added, "Trust me; I saw it at the restaurant. She's never talked to me the way she talked to me that night. I knew then that she was too far gone."

Penny turned to Jaden, "Honey, I don't think I feel like hanging out right now. Can you call me later?"

"Okay," said Jaden. "You guys hang in there; somehow Raine will see the light and come back home."

Nya said, "I hope you're right. I doubt it, but I hope you're right."

Penny stood there as Jaden put his comforting arms around her, "I'll call you later sweetheart."

Penny kissed him, "Okay. I love you."

"I love you too."

He left and Penny sat down on the floor next to her father. She was the oldest daughter and she couldn't save her sister. A year ago the Davis family had a mother, father and three daughters. Now their mother went home with the Lord and the youngest daughter turned her back on them.

Penny sat pondering how she was going to make it right. She knew she couldn't give up trying. She was probably the only one who was going to fight to save her sister but Raine had to realize that she needed to be saved.

Penny decided to go talk with their pastor. Maybe he could shed some light on things. Maybe making all the fuss over the music industry was for nothing. It's possible that they could all be wrong and Raine would be fine. She needed a disinterested third party opinion.

***

Penny arrived at their church where Pastor Dwight Henderson was waiting for her in his office. She knew Pastor Henderson all her life. He baptized her and her sisters as well as all their cousins. He was an honorable man to everyone.

Penny walked in the office and Pastor Henderson offered her a seat. She said, "Thanks Pastor Henderson and thank you for seeing me on such short notice."

Pastor Henderson took his seat, "No problem, Penny; I was wondering if someone was going to talk to me. I have been hearing some things about Raine and I must tell you, I do not like what I'm hearing. But how's your father and Nya? I know the stress of Sunday had to be immense for the family."

"Daddy, well Daddy is trying to make it," said Penny. "We can see the depression all over him and it's understandable. He was with my mother a long time. Nya, I can feel her pain also. She does her best to hide it but I know she's hurting inside."

"What about you baby? You seem to be trying to hold it all together and be strong for everyone."

Penny knew he was right. She had to be stronger than everyone else. They were all crumbling around her. Raine seemed to have lost her mind, her dad was depressed and Nya kept it all inside. She was trying her best to be the glue to hold them all together.

"Pastor, sometimes I cry myself to sleep at night. If it wasn't for Jaden I think I would have lost it also. My sisters are both losing it in different ways and my daddy is depressed most of the time. Now Raine has gone and pushed him over the edge. He wouldn't even talk when I left."

Pastor Henderson shook his head, "I am so sorry to hear all of that. I will continue to pray hard for the Davis family. It seems your entire house is under attack right now."

"Thank you, Pastor."

"I take it you came here to talk about Raine."

Penny sat up in the chair, "Yes sir. She's signed a record deal with Fresh City Records and I'm worried about her. That Damien guy doesn't seem right."

Pastor Henderson sighed, "I wasn't very happy when Derrick brought him into the church but you know we can't turn anyone away. I don't say this often but that's one fella I don't particularity care for either."

"As for Raine and her record deal, it's not a total lost Penny. You see, it's not the singing that's wrong, it's the motive or your actions that make any profession wrong."

"Look at it this way. If I'm going to my job cleaning tables at a strip club and doing my job like I'm suppose then there is no sin against it. I'm not speaking against the word of God nor am I going against any beliefs."

However, if I go to that same job and start telling everyone to have sex outside of marriage, encourage them to use drugs and alcohol well now I'm sinning. It's not the profession; it's my actions within that profession.

"Raine is a singer but she's got to remember that God is first and should never be second. The lyrics that she sings can't go against her Christian beliefs. That's when we have a problem. As a Christian you can work in any profession you like as long as it doesn't go against the tenants of Christianity."

"Remember Penny, we have actors, actresses, singers, producers, athletes, etc. and they are performing their jobs and walking in their faith. Their job is their job but Christianity is their life."

Penny nodded her head, "I think I understand Pastor. It's not the fact that she has a contract but what she does with her life now that she has it."

Pastor Henderson shook his head agreeably, "Yes baby, what's she singing about and what's she doing in her day to day life. Is it edifying God, is it exulting God, is her life giving him all the honor and praise? Those are things that she must be careful of but let me add this one. If she isn't surrounding herself with like-minded people, it's going to be very hard to do those things."

"First Corinthians 15 and 33 tells us to… 'Not be misled: Bad company corrupts good character.' Your sister has good character. I know that because I watched her grow up in my church. I just pray that the company she keeps doesn't corrupt that character."

Penny dropped her head, "I can only pray that it doesn't corrupt her as well Pastor Henderson. Thank you for shedding some light on this battle. I can't give up on my baby sister. I know she'll hate me for butting in but in the end, maybe she'll love me because of the same."

Pastor Henderson stood up to walk her out, "You be strong my young sister. We're all praying for you and the Davis family."

Penny smiled, "Thank you Pastor and good night."

"Good night, baby."

Penny felt better after talking to Pastor Henderson. Maybe Raine would be alright if she kept her sense of decency and morals about herself. She would go home and pray for herself and her family.

Chapter 11

It was close to one in the morning and Raine had fallen off to sleep waiting on Jay to return. She hadn't come up with a plan to tell him anything but one thing for sure, she knew she was not going to tell him what she did with Damien.

Raine was awakened by a deep kiss. This time it was the man she loved. She was happy he had finally arrived. She looked at the clock and said, "It's about time baby; where you been?"

"I told you we had a game in Georgia," said Jay. "You know with travel time it was going to be late; I love you."

Raine smiled. That's something she wanted and needed to hear but like the demons in her dream the visions of Damien and limo were tearing at her mind. She managed to keep smiling, "I love you too, baby."

Jay changed the subject, "So what happened at the audition?"

Raine cringed at the question. The singing was great but the other things were not something she was prepared to share with Jay. She answered, "I got the contract, everyone loved me; I'm going to be a big time singer!"

Jay's head dropped. He clearly didn't want to hear that news.

"What's wrong baby? This will be great for us, you'll see." She wanted someone to be happy for her for a change. Everyone she told her news to wasn't happy. They all thought she was doomed. Yes, she had to endure Damien but now she was going to the top and that's where she wanted to be.

"You know I didn't want that."

Raine's hand hit the couch hard. She said, "Come on Jay, this is my dream and I want to share it with you. I don't try and stand in the way of your basketball."

Jay didn't respond quickly. Raine kissed him and held his head in place. She wanted the kiss to last for an eternity. She wanted Jay to come with her to the studio and be a part of her life. If he did, she would be away from Damien.

Raine asked, "Come to the studio with me baby. It'll be fun."

Jay pulled away from her, "Honey, you know I have school. I can't be at the studio all day with you. I'm only a few months away from my degree and possibly being drafted into the NBA. So are you for that matter. Give this up and finish school. You're right at the finish line."

Raine turned her head to the side. Then she pulled him tightly against her body. She wanted him to make love to her because she knew it would probably be the last time. Of all the bad things she had learned about Damien, one thing he said was becoming true and clear, her family and friends were not going to be there for her so she would be all alone in this new life.

***

Morning came faster than Raine wanted it to come. She slowly got up from the bed and headed for the bathroom. She wasn't happy and dancing like the morning before. She knew this had to be the end for her and Jay.

She was reluctant to leave. In the last two days she realized that she loved Jay with all her heart. Now she was going to leave him to be with a man she despised. She stared at herself in the mirror and suddenly started to cry. The tears kept coming. This was the hardest thing she was going to do in her life.

Jay called to her, "Raine, what's up?"

She quickly got herself together, "Nothing baby; I'm just washing up. I'll be out in a minute."

Jay replied, "Okay, honey."

Raine took a shower and got dressed. When she came out of the bathroom Jay was standing there waiting.

He took her in his arms. Raine asked herself, *'Does he know this is the last time we'll be together?'*

She laid her head on his chest. The emotions quickly built up inside of her and the tears streamed down her face again. She tried to hide it but it wasn't working.

Jay said, "You're not coming back are you? If I don't go with you, I won't see you again."

Raine hesitated to speak. She didn't know how to answer the question except to tell him the truth.

Through her tears she said, "I can't come back. That's why I'm asking you…no begging you to come with me. Please come with me Jay; I love you."

Jay head's hung down, "I have to finish my degree. I can't give up my life for you and it's clear you can't give up yours for me. If we're meant to be then you'll be there for me when I finish my degree."

Raine said, "Or you'll come find me when you finish? It's not a one way street Jay." She cried openly. She knew in her heart that she would not see Jay again. She was making another sacrifice for a music career. This one wasn't illegal or immoral but it hurt worse than any other. She realized at the end that she loved him more than anyone else.

Raine slowly let go of Jay and walked out the door. She didn't look back because that would make it extremely hard for her to leave. She started her car and headed for the studio and her new life as a singer.

Chapter 12

In the three months since Raine signed her contract she found herself in love with Damien. He was nothing like Jay who she thought about from time to time but Damien was moving her music career further than her imagination could have dreamed. For that she felt she owed him and eventually she believed she loved him.

A month ago Damien proposed to Raine and she accepted. She was so excited to be getting married. She believed that if Damien was advancing her career as his girlfriend he would do even more if she was his wife. She was addicted to fame and fortune.

Today was the day that Damien and Raine were set to be married. It was a whirlwind affair and Raine acted like she was excited to become Damien's wife. Inside she questioned her love. The closer she got to this day the more she missed Jay. But, it was too late now. She was going to marry Damien and leave Jay behind.

Raine and Damien were going to be married on the rooftop of the California's most prestigious hotel, the Plaza St. James hotel.

The couple moved from Florida to California shortly after Raine finished laying down the tracks to her first CD. Today she was getting married and tomorrow her CD would be released. The single, "Every Man's Dream" soared up the charts and was predicted to reach number one. Her first song was going to be platinum or better.

Just as Damien told her she was on top of the world and money and fame were coming her way. Everything Damien promised was coming true. She signed a contract in blood but now she was reaping the benefits.

Her new best friend, LaJuan, was with her in the room as she was getting dressed. Raine said, "LaJuan girl, I can't believe this is happening. In three months I'm on top of the world and I'm getting married."

LaJuan said, "Are you sure you want to marry Damien? He treats you mean sometimes."

Raine answered, "Girl he's just stressed sometimes. Later he apologizes and makes it all better, if you know what I mean," Raine smiled a sexy smile.

"Yeah, I know what you mean but I can imagine it getting far worse before it gets better. My sister went through the same thing and her husband almost killed her."

Raine smacked her lips, "That's not going to happen to me. Damien is getting help and we're going to be happy for the rest of our lives." Raine didn't know if that were true or not but it sounded good out loud. She didn't want to talk bad about her soon to be husband. He had his faults but she loved him just the same.

LaJuan said, "Look, just take it from me and keep my number and a couple of others in arms reach. You never know what could happen. My sister called the police just in time. Her husband was about to shoot her when they arrived. Thank God they killed him first."

Raine was shocked, "LaJuan, girl that's not nice."

"Humph, he's dead and my sister isn't getting the living daylights beat out of her anymore. Nice can kiss my behind."

"That's not happening to me, LaJuan. Damien isn't that type of man."

"Keep telling yourself that, okay. I know why you put so much make up on last week. You're not fooling me."

Raine sighed, "Can we please change the subject? This is my day, my special day. I just want to enjoy it please."

LaJuan rolled her eyes, "Okay, not another word about it. You ready to walk that isle? I just hope he doesn't beat your behind at the altar."

Raine put both hands up and reared back, "I can't believe you. Yes…I'm ready. I'm about to be Lorraine Black!"

"Yeah and I feel for you."

"Shut up, LaJuan."

The two women walked to their places. From where Raine stood, she could see the bridesmaids and the groomsmen walking to their respective places. Then the maid of honor and the best man made their walk and it was getting closer to her turn. There were so many people at their ceremony. Some of them were rich and famous. Raine's only wish was that her family could see the light and celebrate this day with her but their relationship had quickly deteriorated over the last three months.

Jay crossed her mind one last time. She wondered what he was doing. She wondered if he had heard the news about her marriage. She thought it was about time for him to graduate from college but she realized that she was right; she would never see him again.

The music turned to the wedding march and Raine nervously started her walk. She had no one to walk her down the aisle so she came down by herself. It focused all the attention on her so she didn't mind at all. She was the center of attention.

Part of her wondered if LaJuan was right. Was she in for a horrible marriage? She blew it off and believed that LaJuan was just jealous. Everyone was always jealous of her and she couldn't understand why.

She got to the altar and there was Damien, smiling. She knew she was making him happy by marrying him. Secretly she wondered if there was anything left in her heart for Jay but she suppressed the thought. Damien was going to be her husband and that was it.

***

Raine was having the time of her life at her wedding reception. She was now a married woman with a soon to be number one single on the charts. Life couldn't be better for her now.

She was in the middle of dancing with her new husband when a commotion was heard from the front entrance. Raine couldn't believe her eyes, it was her big sister Penny.

She ran over to the door, leaving Damien on the dance floor. When she got to the door she paused, wondering what Penny was going to say. She then motioned to the security guards to let her go and she slowly walked over to Penny and they hugged.

For the first time in months Raine felt good about her family, legitimately good. She realized her feelings were real. She wasn't pretending to enjoy the moment. Penny smiled, "We miss you Raine; all of us miss you."

Raine gave a genuine smile, "Even Nya?"

Penny answered, "Especially Nya. We love you, girl."

Raine was really happy, "Come on in girl and have some food and drinks. You can celebrate with me."

"I can't," said Penny. "I just came to tell you that daddy is in the hospital. He had a stroke. I think he really misses you. Please come and see him."

Raine was stunned. She stood with her mouth open not knowing what to say. Her father was the only man on Earth that she truly loved without hesitation. The thought of him lying up in a hospital room was killing her.

She lifted up her dress and ran over to Damien, "Damien, my dad…honey he's in the hospital. I have to go back to Florida."

"It's our wedding day! Not to mention your CD release party is tomorrow. You can't leave now. What will I tell everyone?"

Raine paused. She didn't know what to do. She looked over at Penny, back at Damien and then back to Penny. Penny nodded her head and walked out the room.

Raine took a step but Damien grabbed her by the arm. She looked at him with tears forming in her eyes. Damien whispered, "You better not cry in front of all my family, friends and business associates."

Raine held back the tears and faked a smile. Her thoughts were with her dad but her physical body was hugging Damien. Now she wondered even more if LaJuan was right.

Chapter 13

Penny made it back to Florida without Raine. She hoped and prayed that Raine would have come back to see their father but it didn't work. As she suspected, Damien had total control over her baby sister. The control was to the point of preventing her from coming to see her ill father.

She went straight from the airport to the hospital. When she entered her father's room Nya was sitting by the bed talking to him. Nya asked Penny, "Well, I take it she didn't come back with you?"

Penny answered, "You're right…she stayed with him. Even with Daddy in the hospital, she wouldn't come back home. Damien has complete control over her and I don't like it one bit. I don't know what to do about my baby sister," she cried. Cornelius grabbed her by the hand.

He said, "Pray for Raine, baby. That's all we can do is pray for her. She's too far gone for us earthly soldiers to do anything. We have to turn it all over to God."

Penny replied, "I know, Daddy; I know and I prayed all the way back on the airplane."

Cornelius responded, "Let's pray now."

The ladies agreed. They held each other's hand. Cornelius prayed for his lost daughter and the two daughters who were with him.

Penny couldn't let it go. She was determined to get her sister away from that man. She didn't care how many trips to California or anywhere else in the world she had to go, she was going to keep trying.

After the prayer Jaden came into the room and Penny gave him a big hug. In her research and determination to get her sister back she had neglected her man. Deep inside she knew that had to end.

Penny said, "Hey baby. I'm back from Cali."

Jaden replied, "I see. I just came to see your dad; I didn't think you were home already."

Penny responded, "Well Raine wouldn't listen to me, isn't that a shock? Enough about that, let's go somewhere and spend some time together. I've been neglecting you and that needs to stop."

Jaden smiled, "Sounds good to me. Mr. Davis, you okay?"

Cornelius answered, "I'm doing fine. You guys go and have fun."

Nya added, "Yeah Penny, go and have fun. I got Daddy, but tomorrow it's your turn girl."

Penny took Jaden by the arm, "Thanks Daddy. I got you Nya; I'll be by tomorrow."

"Cool," said Nya.

Cornelius replied, "Bye, baby."

Penny replied, "Bye, Daddy." The couple walked out the room and out of the hospital. For one day Penny was going to forget about all the problems she was experiencing with her family and enjoy some time with her man.

They went to a nice restaurant and then back to Jaden's place. Penny walked in first and headed straight to the bedroom. Jaden asked, "Baby, where you going so fast?"

"If you have to ask maybe I should come back."

Jaden ran up behind her and grabbed her by the waist. Like a school girl Penny giggled, turned and kissed him. She then broke away, ran and dived on the bed. Jaden was right behind her.

Penny was enjoying her time with Jaden and the evening was just about to start. Love was in the air and she was enjoying it. For one night she didn't think of Raine, or anything else. She just focused on her and Jaden.

***

Penny felt the morning sun warmly caressing her face. Jaden moved next to her and put his arms around her. She smiled. Last night was great and she didn't want to get up. She thought, *'Sure fornication is a sin but no one is perfect.'*

Penny turned around in the bed and smiled at Jaden. He returned that knowing smile of love they developed over the years. They were both twenty-seven and had been together for twelve years.

They met in high school. Jaden was on the football team and Penny was a cheerleader. Everyone in school believed they would be the perfect couple and time had proved them right. Penny couldn't imagine being with anyone else but Jaden.

She said, "When I was at Raine's reception, I thought about the day we would marry. I would want all of my family there to share my day with me. I don't understand how she could get married without anyone from her family being there. To me that's so sad."

Jaden replied, "I don't understand it either baby. Your sister spun out of control when your mother died and it got worse over the last year. I don't know how she could not come back to see her father. There would be nothing on earth more important to me than coming back to see my dad."

Penny inched closer to him, "I know baby; if ever I go that way, slap me."

Jaden laughed, "Okay, remember you said that."

Penny laughed with him and then they kissed. Every kiss felt better than the previous one.

Jaden pulled away and reached in his night stand. Penny got ready. She knew he was reaching for a condom. He moved back next to her and said, "Penny, will you marry me?"

Penny was so excited that she almost knocked Jaden off the bed. This was the day she dreamed of for the last two years. She had only one answer in her heart, "Yes, baby; I will marry you, yes!"

Jaden hugged his new fiancé and she hugged him back as tight as she could. She couldn't wait to get to the hospital and tell Nya and her dad.

Penny jumped up and grabbed her clothes. Jaden asked, "Hey, where you going so fast?"

Penny answered, "To the hospital to tell Daddy and Nya."

Jaden said, "Huh; I thought maybe we could do a little something to celebrate?"

She froze, then threw her clothes to the floor and hoped on top of Jaden. She loved him and now she was going to be his wife. Life was great. She seductively licked her lips, "You just lay there and let me handle this."

Jaden simply said, "Okay."

***

When Jaden and Penny got to the hospital Nya was drinking coffee in the hallway. Nya greeted them, "Good morning lovebirds."

Penny flashed her left hand so Nya could see the ring. They both shouted in the hospital.

Jaden said, "Hey guys, we're in the hospital."

All the nurses were looking at them. Penny said, "Oops, sorry."

Nya laughed and then hugged her big sister, "I am so happy for you guys. Praise the Lord, something good for a change."

Jaden said, "Amen."

Nya grabbed Jaden, "Welcome to the family!"

"Thanks Nya. How's your dad?"

Nya answered, "He's doing fine. They're thinking about letting him go tomorrow. That is if he continues to recover."

Penny said, "Well, I have to go tell him the news." She rushed into the hospital room where she saw two of her aunties and her uncle laughing and joking with her dad. She was happy that he was doing well.

Penny said, "Daddy, I got some news."

Cornelius replied, "About Raine?"

Penny's heart almost dropped but she decided to dismiss it. She knew her dad loved Raine and missed her very much.

"No Daddy about me; I'm getting married." She flashed her ring and a big smile.

Cornelius reached out to hug his oldest daughter. She hugged her father as hard as she could. Nothing was more important than making him happy.

Her aunts and uncle hugged and congratulated her as well. Jaden came in the room and got the same reception. For once, the Davis family had reason to celebrate.

After visiting hours ended at the hospital, Penny came home. She was by herself because it was Nya's turn to be out on a date. It was close to midnight when the phone rang. To her amazement, it was Raine.

Penny picked up the phone, "Raine, is that you, girl, please tell me you're in town?"

Raine cleared her throat, "I can't tell you that sis. I'm still in California. My CD release party is tonight. That's why I couldn't come back with you. I hope everyone understands. My life won't let me just pick up and go anymore."

Penny was sad, "You put that over coming to see your father? You could have postponed it a few days. What if the worse had happened? Then you would have never gotten to see him alive again." Raine didn't answer and Penny decided to calm down and try to be hospitable. She didn't want Raine to hang up the phone and miss an opportunity to talk to her sister.

She continued, "Well, Daddy's doing much better now. They're even thinking of letting him go tomorrow."

Raine responded, "That's great." Penny thought she heard sniffing. Raine continued, "I'm glad to hear that. Penny, I just couldn't leave my wedding to come home. Why can't you understand that?"

Penny's eyes looked sad, "I can't Raine. Not when it comes to Daddy. He's the only parent we have left and we almost lost him. You didn't even invite us to the wedding. We found out on TV that you were getting married. That's no way to treat your family."

Silence filled the airwaves. Penny found herself trying to calm down again. She was afraid that Raine hung up the phone.

She decided to ask, "So…how's married life, I mean all one day of it?

Raine giggled. Penny was happy to hear that Raine was still on the line and she even laughed a bit.

Raine answered, "Well, so far so good. Everyone keeps telling me I made a mistake. That's not too comforting but I'm getting used to it."

Penny didn't want to get into it so she decided to change the conversation a bit and tell her the news, "You know Jaden proposed to me this morning and I said, yes."

"What? You're getting married? Oh my goodness girl, I'm so happy for you; I wanna come."

Penny was excited, "I want you there baby girl, you know it."

Raine calmed down, "I'll have to check my schedule. Now that my CD is out, I'll be going on this big tour. Everyone is getting me ready for it. You just can't imagine what I do on a day-to-day basis."

Penny thought, *'And she shifts the conversation right back to her. Some things never change.'* Penny said, "I can't imagine."

Raine asked, "You still tearing things up at church?"

"Yeah, you know I love to sing for the Lord, so I'm going to keep standing firm on holy ground. Gospel is my heart and I won't do anything else."

"Maybe I can help you get into that area."

"Raine, I'm not about all that. I love singing in church and that's the extent of it. Me and Jaden, we're just going to have a nice quiet family lifestyle like mom and dad. I don't want the big stage or big lights. Even in the gospel arena. I'm just not like you."

"I guess I'm the only one, huh?"

"Raine, you don't know how much I want you to safely live out your dream. I love you girl but I don't and never have gotten a good feeling from Damien."

Raine was quiet. Penny continued, "Are you okay; really...are things okay?"

Raine started to answer but was cut off by someone in the background. Penny asked, "Raine?"

Raine's voice shifted, "Penny, I have to go. They're calling me to get ready for the release party."

"Okay girl," said Penny. "Please...please call me if you need to. Hell, call me just because. I'm here anytime, day or night."

"Thanks Penny. Bye, big sis."

"It was great talking to you Raine. Bye, sweetie."

Raine said softly, "It was great. Bye, bye."

Penny hugged the phone like it was her baby sister. She missed her so much. She was arrogant, conceited and spoiled but she loved her just the same.

She hung the phone up and grabbed another piece of clothing to fold. She sat there quietly, deep in thought about everything from her mom's death to her marriage proposal. She thought about Pastor Henderson saying that the Davis family was under attack and he was right. It seemed they just couldn't escape pain and heartache but at least no one else had died. She couldn't have taken it if she lost her dad.

Chapter 14

Raine hung up the phone and turned to Damien. He looked angry and she was scared. She said, "Damien, I just wanted to hear from home one time before my big night. Please don't be mad. You know my dad is in the hospital."

He just stared coldly at Raine. She hoped he would just leave the room and not hit her again.

He turned back around, "I told you to forget home. Your life is here with me, not back there. Don't cross me again."

She said, "Why can't I talk to my family?"

The open hand slap hit her so hard that she nearly flipped over. She didn't have the strength to get up. She stayed there, on the floor, hoping that would be the extent of it. On the biggest night of her career she had to endure another beating. She thought, *'Why did I marry this man?"*

Damien sternly shouted and pointed at her, "Look what you made me do! I told you not to contact them and I mean it. Your place is here!" He reached down and pulled her up by the throat, "Don't make me repeat myself."

Her tone was meek, "Okay Damien. Okay baby, I won't call again, I promise...I promise." He let go and she lay back on the floor, holding back the tears. She didn't want to mess up her makeup.

She heard the loud sounding slam of the hotel door. She was glad it wasn't worse. She pulled herself up to the bed and looked herself over.

She heard the door open again and fear overcame her. She looked at the bathroom and thought she could make it in there before he came back in the room.

"Raine, oh my God girl; what did that jerk do to you this time."

It was LaJuan. Raine was happy to see her. She hugged her tightly and cried on her shoulder. LaJuan was her best friend and the only one she could trust. She knew LaJuan wouldn't do anything to hurt her and she could count on her anytime.

She held LaJuan by the shoulders and looked her square in the eyes, "LaJuan, I need you to do something for me."

"What girl? You know I'll do anything for you; just name it."

Raine tried to get herself together, "I know I'm not going make it. I can't keep taking this and Damien said that if I try and get out of this contract those people will kill me. I want to set up a bank account and an insurance policy so when I die, my family will be taken care of for sure."

"Girl, don't talk like that."

"You were right; I shouldn't have married him. In just one day he's getting worse. He won't even let me see my family."

Damien shouted, "Raine...get out here, we're ready for you."

Both ladies jumped from the bass in his voice. Raine answered, "Coming Damien."

They came to the outer room. Some men in suits walked into the room. They looked sharply at Damien. Raine saw this man who professed to be strong and tough suddenly turn meek and submissive. She wished the men would stay around all the time.

Damien said, "Raine, go on out to the party. Anthony will introduce you." He looked at LaJuan, "What the heck are you staring at? Get your leaching behind out of here."

Raine and LaJuan left the room but before she did she heard Damien pleading about something. Whatever was wrong, she hoped she wouldn't have to take a beating for it.

LaJuan said, "I bet his behind is in trouble now."

Raine replied, "How do you know?"

"I have a friend who has friends. I just made a call and they made a call. Eventually it got to people who he answers to."

Raine stopped in her tracks, "LaJuan, you're gonna get me killed."

"Don't worry girl. He'll be in check for a while."

Raine looked strangely at LaJuan. Her friend hadn't shown this side of herself before. Did she know something that Raine didn't? She didn't have time to think about it. Instead she needed to make her grand entrance into her release party.

Raine got herself together and listened as she was being introduced. Damien was the worst part of this experience for her but all the recording and singing was the best. She lived for the moments when she became the center of attention and he couldn't get his hands on her. She was paying a high price for the fame but these moments were what she lived for.

When her name was announced she came out waving and smiling like nothing happened. No one in the room would ever know the trials she endured; no one except LaJuan.

Everyone yelled, "Raine, Raine..." She loved it.

"Thank you everyone. I am so proud to be here tonight to introduce you to my new CD entitled 'Let it Raine'. There are so many people to thank for this moment that it would be impossible to name them all, but for sure I need to thank my husband, Damien Black and everyone at Fresh City Records for their kindness, support and most of all, their patience."

"I would also be remised if I didn't thank my best friend in the whole world… LaJuan Craig, for all she has done for me. Isn't she the best y'all?" She clapped and the entire room joined in and clapped. LaJuan waved at the crowd.

"Now let's start to play that CD so everyone can enjoy it! Woo hoo!"

Raine had forgotten everything that happened in her hotel room. Each time she had to endure a beating she learned how to forget it and keep going. She would have made a fabulous actress.

The party was in high gear and she loved every minute of it. On the other side of the room she saw Damien talking to the same men. He appeared very humble, bowing to their every word. LaJuan stood with them now and she didn't look intimidated at all. Raine suspected something but she didn't know what it was and she dared not ask.

Raine shook hands with everyone in attendance but one man caught her attention over everyone. The man said, "Hey, you didn't thank God like most R&B singers do."

    Raine just smiled, shook his hand and kept moving. She didn't think of God at all. In fact she hadn't even thought of God, Jesus or church since she signed her contract in blood. The comment quickly faded as everyone continued to pay attention to her.

Chapter 15

LaJuan Craig was an alluring, mysterious soul who knew how to control situations and motivate those around her to do what she needed them to do. She was charged by the men in suits to watch Raine and make sure she stayed on track. However, it was Damien who she came to hate and admire.

She arrived at her office; the office where only a select few knew the location. She pulled her brand new candy apple red Lexus into the garage and handed the guard the keys. She didn't even bother looking at him or speaking to him. She did note his lust for her as she swayed to the elevator. Once inside, she saw the guard still looking and blew him a kiss. The doors closed and she laughed, knowing she made his day.

She arrived at her private office and placed her personal items down. She proceeded to the main conference room where the men waited. They wanted to know the status of things at Fresh City Records and where Raine's head was at.

She started, "Gentlemen, as I told you last night, Damien is becoming a problem. He's beating Raine. I know we have allowed him some latitude in this area in the past but this time, I don't believe we should."

"As you know we have a talent in Raine Davis and we would be foolish to let Damien ruin it. I suggest we ring him in, maybe even end our relationship with him…permanently."

The room was quiet while the men in suits conferred. LaJuan stood there looking sexy in her short purple and black dress. Her hair was styled just perfectly down to her shoulders. She boasted a coco colored skin with no marks of any kind.

When they were done the leader spoke, "We understand the situation with Damien but we cannot end our relationship with him just yet. Instead we will teach him a lesson. We will teach him not to damage our product."

LaJuan was not happy with that decision but she knew better then to cross her bosses, "I understand. I will continue to watch Raine and report back to you. Oh and you should know that she believes Damien will kill her one day. She asked me to set up a bank account and insurance policy so her family would be taken care of."

The leader asked, "What will alleviate all of her fears?"

LaJuan answered, "Allow her to go see her family. For some stupid reason Damien is afraid to let her go home. She needs something from her family. A trip home will help her greatly."

The leader looked to the man next to him and said, "See to it." The man didn't utter a word. He stood up and left the room.

LaJuan asked, "Will that be all?"

The leader answered, "You may go."

LaJuan turned and walked out of the conference room. She commanded respect throughout the building. She returned to her car and headed off. Her job for the day was done.

Chapter 16

Penny woke up the next morning after hearing Nya singing in the kitchen. She went in to see her, "So how was the date, any potential there?"

"He was a jerk...a jerk with money but still a jerk."

"O-M-G, just hang in there girl, love will come your way."

Nya rolled her eyes, "I'm not that concerned. I'm just twenty-six years old and have plenty of time. Right now, my priority is my master's degree and a good job, girl. I'm not Raine honey."

"I heard that. I should go back to school myself but now that I'm getting married...did you see my ring?"

Nya laughed, "Yes girl, I saw it a thousand times yesterday, okay."

Penny got serious, "Raine called last night. She seemed up and down in her feelings."

Nya face turned serious, "She called here…last night? You didn't pass out?"

"No girl, I didn't. We talked for a bit before she said she had to go for her party. I know everything isn't as perfect as she would want us to believe."

Nya said, "I know it isn't either. I've seen reports on TV about that Damien guy. He's no good. Did you hear about Elaine, his so called last star?"

"Yeah, she's broke and on the street; what a shame."

Nya changed the subject, "What time you going to the hospital?"

"I think about ten. Are they going to release him?"

Nya took the bacon off the grill and placed it on Penny's plate, "I think so but someone will have to sit with him all the time until he gets his strength back. We can take shifts. I know Auntie Rose and Aunt Bea will chip in as well."

"That sounds good to me. I'm meeting Jaden for dinner at seven so I can watch him until then."

Nya said, "Cool, then I will go to work and leave it all to my big sis." She smiled and walked out with her plate, high-fiving Penny on the way.

Penny grabbed her plate and sat at the table sipping on her coffee. The smell of the freshly cooked bacon, eggs and pancakes made her hungry and Nya's cooking was just what she needed.

All the time she thought about her baby sister. Hearing her voice the night before made her feel good. She wished they could talk more but at least she got that opportunity.

She decided that today was going to be a good day. She couldn't do anything for Raine but she was going to bring her daddy home and make sure he was happy and well taken care of before her date.

She admired her new ring and thought about what dress she was going to wear that evening. She wanted it to be perfect for her man. Her first bite into breakfast was passionate. Nya was the best cook in the house and she didn't let her down.

Chapter 17

Raine woke up feeling better than she had in months. Her CD release party went better than she expected and she didn't have any more issues with Damien. She thought, *'Whatever LaJuan did must have worked. I have to admit, I'm curious but I'm more grateful to have some peace.'*

She looked at Damien as he slept. She shivered at the thought of stabbing him in his sleep. She knew that was something she could never do but she did think about it.

When he wasn't angry, he was great. Not as good as Jay, but still he was tolerable. Her issue with him was his temper and he took it out on her physically and emotionally.

Damien woke up and saw Raine staring at him, "What's wrong, baby?"

Raine smiled, "Nothing; nothing at all. I was just thinking about last night and how great my party was." She turned and looked in the mirror to cover her lying. She was really thinking about killing him. If she was brave enough, she would have done it. She decided to push her luck, "Before I go on tour, I'd like to go home and see my family."

Damien slammed the cover off of him and stood up. Raine jumped and prepared to get hit again. She wondered if she was becoming immune to the beatings. She got scared and eased away from him.

Damien took a step toward her but his phone rang. It was the ringtone that Raine believed was from the mysterious men Damien deals with. He rushed to answer it like his life depended on it.

After a few moments he came back in the room and she got scared again. She thought, *'If he hits me again, I'm leaving him. I don't care if it's in a box, I'm leaving.'*

She noticed a change. His anger appeared to be gone. He said, "Okay, we'll make it happen. You can go back to Florida and visit your family. You just remember that they will try and lure you back in that mundane life."

Raine was shocked. She now knew LaJuan had something to do with the men in suits. She must have said something to them about how she was being treated. Whatever the case she was going to go home and see her family. For that she was truly grateful.

She replied, "I'll remember Damien and they won't pull me back into that life. I like singing on the big stage and that won't change. What I don't like is the beatings." She didn't want to make eye contact with him out of fear that she would make him mad.

He said, "I'm sorry for my temper Raine. I love you. I love you more than any woman I've ever met in my life. I just want you to listen to me and do what I say. You don't know what I know about this business and this life. I'm just trying to help you. I only have your best interest in mind."

Raine begged, "I do listen to you Damien but I don't need to be slapped and beaten to understand. I'm the star here and if you mess up my looks people won't like me."

She felt really brave now. Raine didn't know how far she could go with this but she was going to use this opportunity to speak her mind. She felt like she could be a star without Damien. She was big enough to cut the leash and maybe this was her opportunity to push back a little. In her mind she believed the men in suits were calling all the shots so why did she need Damien?

Damien sternly looked at her, "So you think you're in control now. You think that because you have a hit single, which I wrote by the way, and a large following that you think you're the boss." He paced the floor shaking his head, pondering his next move.

Damien stopped in front of Raine and pointed his finger in her face, "Don't push your luck."

He walked in the bathroom and slammed the door behind him. Raine stood there in panic mode. She married this man two days before but she wanted out of it now. She was scared of him and what he might do to her or her family.

Raine's cell phone rang. The caller ID said "LaJuan". She quickly answered it, "Hey girl."

"Hey, you up already?"

Raine quickly forgot her fear, "Yeah, I was so hyped up that I couldn't sleep. Guess what, Damien is letting me go home before the tour."

"Letting you? Girl you're the star, don't pay him any attention. He wants you to think he's in charge."

"He is my husband, LaJuan."

"Yeah, that was a mistake."

"LaJuan stop." Raine didn't like being reminded of how LaJuan felt about Damien. She wasn't happy with the situation but she didn't need to hear it all the time.

"LaJuan asked, "Can you do breakfast?"

"I don't know; Damien is in the bathroom. I'll see and let you know; okay?"

"Cool, see you girl."

"Hey I didn't know you knew those suits like that. I saw you talking to them last night. You've been hiding stuff from me."

There was a slight pause on the phone, "Raine some things shouldn't be talked about okay. You're my girl and I love you but please don't go there."

Raine was puzzled, "Okay...well I will leave it alone but I will thank you. I believe you had something to do with Damien's change of attitude towards me."

"Yeah, bye Raine."

"Bye."

Chapter 18

Raine left to meet LaJuan for breakfast and Damien sat on the hotel bed. He was fuming. His manhood had been challenged by his new bride. No woman had ever spoken to him like that and gotten away with it.

He remembered how his father handled things when he was growing up. His father would have shut that talk down in a minute, so why couldn't he? Did his fear of the men in the suits become so great that he would allow a woman to walk all over him? This had to stop. He had to put an end to her disrespect of him. He paced the floor planning his next moves. He didn't care what the consequences would be but he was going to put her in check.

His boy Don came to the room and Damien let him in, "What's up, Don?"

"Hey what's up, bro? That party last night was off the chain. Did you see me hook up with that sweet redbone girl? I don't even remember her name. I just promised her a contract and got me some. They still fall for that mess."

Damien didn't answer. He clearly was preoccupied.

Don said, "Hey brother, what's up?"

"Oh, yeah I saw you hook up with that girl at the party. My mind is just on Raine and her actions. I'm letting her go back home before the tour."

"What? You're not afraid of her family trying to talk her into quitting?"

"No, she knows she can't quit but she might come to realize that she doesn't need me anymore. The group will make her a star with or without me. The sooner she realizes that I bow to them she'll dump me and I won't be able to do anything about it. They'll back her not me. Besides they're forcing me to do it."

"What they told you, to let her go home? Anyway, you have a contract. She can't leave you."

"Yeah they told me to let her go home. I didn't have a choice in the matter." Damien stared right through his friend, "Do you think that contract will matter to them? If she wants to dump me they will do it for her and they will move me out of the way or worse, I will mysteriously disappear. You know what I mean?"

Don leaned against the dresser, "Yeah, I do. Wow, what are you going to do?"

"It's time to start getting her hooked on crack. I'll do it slowly at first and then more and more until she's afraid to leave me. She'll be so dependent on the crack that she won't think about leaving. I'll have to contain myself until she's hooked, keep my temper in check. I might need some help with that bro."

"I got you man. You know I'm here for you. I can contact our connections and make a purchase but how are you going to get her to use it."

"She's developed a taste for alcohol, so I'll be as sweet as I can to her then when she's drunk enough, I'll introduce her to it. She won't even know she's using, until it's too late."

"Cool...I'll get it started."

"Thanks man. You've always got my back and I won't forget it. You know this tour is about to fill our pockets with more cash than ever."

Don rubbed his hands together, "Yeah boy, I can't wait to get started. When is she going home?"

"I got her on the private jet scheduled to leave today. She'll be back on Monday. That will give us about a week to get ready for the tour. Since she wants to leave, I'll have me a little fun while she's gone as well. I'll need something to take my mind off of my wife."

They both laughed, knowing what Damien was referring to without speaking it. Don said, "Sounds good. I'll check you later, bro."

"Cool. By the way, how was the redbone?"

"Sweet, but she can't sing worth nothing. She's pretty upset this morning when I kicked her out without a deal."

They high-fived each other and Damien said, "That's how you work brother."

Don walked out the room and Damien sat down and smiled. Because of the men in the suits he had to do things differently. He was going to get Raine strung out on crack then she would treat him like a god just to get that next high.

As for right now he was planning on who he was going to get with while Raine was gone. He reasoned that he might as well enjoy the company of another woman while she was away. It was her fault for leaving.

Chapter 19

Raine was excited. She was finally on the record company's private jet heading home to Florida. She smiled from ear to ear as she imagined that she was going to be able to spend some time with her family, and see her ailing father again. The issues she had with them before she left seemed like ancient history to her now. All she wanted to do was get back home and hug them all as tightly as she could.

Even after all the issues with the family she still found herself missing her nemesis, Nya. When she got off the plane she was going to hug Nya tighter than all of them and tell her how much she loved her. What she wasn't going to talk about was her relationship with Damien.

She knew if she discussed anything negative then her family, especially Penny, would gnaw on it like a dog with a bone. She loved Penny but Penny always wanted to be the protector. She loved her for it but she felt Penny didn't know when to stop.

During the limo ride home, she grew more and more excited. As she passed the neighborhood store that she went to growing up, she smiled. It brought back such fond memories of her childhood. Many of them were with her sisters, running around in the streets, just being happy kids. She thought, *'What happened to those days? Since momma died we haven't been the same.'*

The limo pulled up in front of the house where she grew up. So many memories flooded her mind. It made her realize how much she missed everyone. She remembered calling her home a "dump" and regretted it so much now. It wasn't a dump, it was home and it would always be home. All of her subconscious dreams were of this place. It was not and never would be a dump. It was a palace where she will always long to return. No matter how far she goes away she would always find a way home.

A tear came down as she remembered her mother and all the fond times they spent together. She had only been gone for a short while so it surprised her that she missed everything so much. The pain and misery of the new life she was living obviously made her miss home more than she knew.

The driver opened the limo door but she had to pause before getting out. Coming home for the first time was not going to be easy but she had to do it. She had to gain something back of what she lost. She wasn't sure what that something was, but she needed to be here, now. She slowly stepped out of the limo. As soon as she was fully out of the limo she saw Penny and Nya running out of the house towards her. The sisters embraced each other with so much love it lit up the streets for miles around.

Raine tightly held both her sisters at once. She loved them so much and missed them even more. She said, "Nya, I know we have had our differences but I missed you so much. I guess I miss fighting with you." They both laughed.

Nya replied, "Girl, I missed you too and I must say you rocking that video. I'm so proud of you."

Raine responded, "Awe...well you did teach me how to dance."

Penny said, "What, I taught both of y'all how to dance and sing so what's up with that?"

Raine hugged Penny again, "Yes, you did big sis and I love you too. I love both of you guys so much." Tears welled up in all their eyes, "I didn't fully realize how much until this moment."

Penny replied, "I love you too, baby girl."

Nya added, "Yeah, me too."

Penny put her arm around Raine, "Come on inside. Daddy just got home from the hospital today. He'll be so glad to see you."

Raine found herself filled with excitement as she entered the Davis house again. She saw Cornelius' favorite chair had been replaced with a wheelchair. Sadness overpowered the excitement.

"Daddy," She ran over and hugged her father. He smiled, laughed and nearly came to tears to see his baby girl again. "Daddy, I miss you so much." She kissed him on the cheek.

"Baby girl, where you been? I haven't seen you in years."

Raine looked at her sisters. Nya said, "He's lost some memory."

Raine almost cried. In all the excitement of coming home she didn't realize that her father wasn't looking in the best of health. She always remembered her father being a tall, strong man, ripping with muscles. To her and her sisters he was superman but now he had lost weight and he could hardly hold his head up.

"Daddy, I've just been gone a few months." She hugged him so tightly and he laughed with happiness while she secretly cried. Her dad had lost some of his precious memories and she couldn't help but blame herself.

She looked up at her sisters with pleading eyes, "Is he gonna get better?"

Penny answered, "We don't know. For now all we can do is pray and hope for the best."

***

Raine woke up to the fresh Florida breeze coming through her bedroom window. She removed the screen and stuck her head out the window so the breeze would blow on her face. It felt so good. It was just like she always remembered. California was nice but it wasn't Florida. The Florida sun was hot but when the breeze hit right, there was nothing like it. She missed so much about home.

Raine and her sisters stayed up for hours talking. That was something they had not done since the loss of their mother. They talked about so many memories of events that happened in their childhood. Some of which Raine had even forgotten. She loved them so much but they just couldn't agree on one thing, their professional careers.

Raine was happy to hear that Pastor Henderson didn't disapprove of her profession but if he knew that she was drinking and fornicating, he would not approve of that. She even used marijuana a couple times to take the edge off. She thought if Damien knew, he would kill her but sometimes the stress was too much for her, so she tried it.

Anytime Penny or Nya started asking about Damien or her personal life she managed to shift the conversation to something else. She knew they knew she was being abused but she didn't want to talk about that. She believed LaJuan had an impact somehow and the abuse would be over so she didn't want to talk about it.

She wanted to indulge Penny and Nya in conversation that would keep them laughing and loving each other. She didn't want to argue with them.

She brought her head back inside the window and the smell of home cooked country breakfast engulfed her and overpowered her senses. Homemade Davis breakfast was just what the doctor ordered. She couldn't get it anywhere else but in that house. That bacon, eggs, grits and pancakes was something she missed. She loved the way they fried their eggs and laid them over the grits. There was no place where she could get it made this way.

She threw on her robe and walked toward the kitchen. She smiled when she saw her dad sitting in the dining room. She immediately went over to hug and kiss him, "Good morning Daddy; I love you soooooo much." She could never get enough of hugging her daddy.

Cornelius said, "Hey baby girl, when did you get home?"

Raine dropped her head on his shoulder. It was killing her to see her father who was always sharp, now suffering so much, "Last night Daddy." She kissed him on the cheek again.

Cornelius replied, "Ohhh, it's so good to see you again. You look just like your momma. Where is Diane?"

Raine said, "Yes Daddy; It's good to see you too." Through her tears she said, "Momma…momma's not here Daddy."

Cornelius said, "Oh, okay baby."

Raine walked into the kitchen. Penny was flipping pancakes as only she could. That act brought more memories back for Raine. To Raine it was Penny who looked like their mom and it brought a chill to Raine.

Raine smiled at Penny, "Good morning love. Flip one of them cakes over here. I'm starving!"

Penny smiled back and hugged her sister, "Good morning baby girl. How'd you sleep?"

Raine answered, "I slept better than I have in months. There's no bed like the bed I grew up sleeping on. Oh and not to mention that fresh morning air. Oh my God, there's nothing like it."

Penny said, "Well you welcome to stay forever."

Raine smiled, "Come Penny, don't go there okay."

Penny handed her a plate, "Okay; you ready to eat?"

Raine rubbed her hands together, "Oh yeah. The smell woke me up. I'm 'bout to destroy this mess."

***

Raine, Penny and Nya all decided to go the mall and do some shopping. Raine had plenty of money in her bank account now, more than she ever believed possible. She wanted to buy something for her sisters but wondered if they would take it.

Raine popped in the dressing room to try on a dress while her sisters were still shopping. Her back was to the door as she took off her dress to try on a new one. Before she knew it, Nya popped opened the dressing room door and Raine turned quickly to hide her back. It wasn't quick enough.

Nya's mouth dropped as she stared at her sister, "Raine, what happened?"

Raine quickly put on the dress, "Nothing, I just fell during rehearsal." She situated the dress on her body, rubbing it up and down like she was pressing it. She gave a fake smile to Nya, "So how does it look."

She knew Nya wasn't buying her excuse but she didn't want to talk about her personal life.

Nya said, "It looks nice on you and it covers your bruises."

Raine folded her arms. She couldn't look at Nya, "I…I fell on the stage…really, that's all it was, a trip and fall. I need to change back now. Please don't tell Penny. I just want to enjoy my time here…okay?"

Nya didn't say anything. She backed out the dressing room and closed the door. Raine hoped Nya wouldn't tell Penny. She didn't want anything to start between them. She sat on the bench of the dressing room and tried to suppress her tears.

***

The incident at the mall had passed and Nya either didn't tell Penny or Penny decided not to say anything about it. Raine was just glad it was over. She didn't try on anymore clothes while they were shopping. She was happy that she had the opportunity to spoil her sisters with some new clothes. It shocked her that they freely accepted her gifts but she didn't complain about it. She was just happy she could do it.

Raine was enjoying her vacation with her family. Her heart was hurt over her father but there was nothing she could do about it. She just showed him the most love she could.

All the sisters gathered together to make dinner. Penny wanted to celebrate her engagement while her baby sister was in town. The three sisters, Jaden and Cornelius were seated at the dinner table. Jaden blessed the food and everyone dug into it.

"Raine, I am so happy you're here," said Penny. Today has been great with breakfast, shopping and last night all the bonding over memories. Girl, I missed you so much."

Raine replied, "I feel the same big sis. I've been so engaged in making music and building my marriage and career that I forgot about my family. I needed this so much before my tour. I hope you guys come to my concert. I told them they better schedule a stop near my home so my family can see me on stage."

Nya didn't speak. She just sat quietly, eating her dinner and helping her dad. Penny expressed excitement, "We'll be there, won't we Nya?"

Nya never stopped feeding her dad. She ignored them, not paying any attention.

Jaden tapped Raine on her shoulder, "I'll be…"

Raine flinched in pain and grabbed her shoulder. Jaden apologized, "I'm sorry."

Penny moved over to Raine and pulled back her dress. She saw the nasty bruise on Raine's shoulder that Nya saw earlier.

Penny shouted, "What the heck is that?"

Nya stood up, "Penny calm down, remember Daddy is here." She pointed at their dad.

Raine jumped up from the table, "Like I told Nya, I fell during rehearsal. It's nothing. Just leave me alone." She ran into her bedroom and flopped down on the bed. All the fun came crashing to an end. She thought she could hide the bruises but she couldn't.

There was a knock at her door. Raine didn't want to answer it. She figured it was Penny poised and ready to judge her and tell her how right she was about Damien.

The knock came again. Raine got up and slowly answered the door. It was Nya. This surprised her because she still thought Nya was her nemesis.

Nya walked in the room, "I haven't even been in this room since you left. I couldn't bring myself to come in here."

Raine cracked a smile, "Really? I thought you would have changed it around, made it into a family room or something; anything to celebrate me being gone."

She looked lovingly into Raine's eyes, "Raine, I love you. I know I haven't shown it in the past and maybe I was a bit jealous but in the end you are my sister and nothing will ever change that. I can't accept the fact that you fell. I've seen this before with my friend Francis. Her boyfriend beat the hell out of her every chance he got. It looks the same, Raine."

Raine squirmed, shifting her weight from side to side, "He's not beating me. He gets mad and losses his temper but he loves me. We have a great relationship and sometimes I mouth off to him. You know how it is, Nya."

Nya nodded her head, "No Raine, that's not love and it's never your fault. You don't show someone love by beating them so badly that a bruise is on them. Jaden didn't even touch you that hard. You're acting just like Francis, you're in denial baby."

Raine replied, "He does love me…and I love him. Like I said I just need to control my mouth sometimes. You, of all people, know how I can be."

Penny walked in the room. Raine took a deep breath, "Don't start Penny. I really don't want to hear it. Really, I don't okay?"

"I was just going to tell you your food is getting cold and Daddy wants us all at the table. He even keeps asking for mom."

Raine dried the tears in her eyes. Nya hugged her and walked out the room. Raine tried to walk out but Penny stepped in her way and hugged her tightly. She whispered in her ear, "I'm here for you, baby girl. I'm here for you." Penny turned and walked away. Raine was pleased she didn't say anything else about the bruise. She knew Penny was trying so she would continue to try as well.

***

It was Sunday morning and the Davis household was busy getting breakfast and dressed for church. Raine hadn't been to their church in so long that she longed to go back. She didn't know if they would let her sing but she just wanted to be in the house.

Raine studied her naked body in the mirror. The bruises were slowly diminishing. The worse one was on her shoulder and it was still black-and-blue. Her dress would cover it but she hoped no one would touch it. It still caused her some pain.

She washed up and put on her makeup and clothes. She walked out to the living room and stopped dead in her tracks. She couldn't look him in the face but she managed to say, "Jay…what are you doing here?"

Jay walked over to her and took her into his arms. It felt great to be in his arms again. She had forgotten how good she felt when she was with him. Her heart tingled with love but guilt soon took over and she pushed him away, "I can't do this. I'm a married woman now, Jay."

Jay pulled her chin towards him so she would look him in the eyes, "I know you married him but I also know that I'm the one you love. I felt it just now. You know that same feeling I felt when we hugged months ago. I know you felt my love for you too. You can't deny it."

Raine looked out of the corner of her eye. She saw her sisters standing in the other room watching them. She knew they put this together. They believed by bringing Jay to the house, Raine would consider leaving Damien and her new life behind.

She patted Jay on the chest, "I can't do this, Jay. No matter what I may feel or what I'm going through, being with you is not the right thing to do. It's a line I can't…no won't cross. I love my husband and I won't do this. I'm sorry."

Jay replied, "I'm not asking you to do anything or cross any line. I just came by to see you before you leave. I just wanted to tell you that I still love you."

Tears formed in Raine's eyes. She knew she had to leave now. She turned to her sisters, "Are we ready to go?" She wanted to respond kindly to Jay but she knew that wouldn't be right. She did still love him but she couldn't say it out loud.

Penny stepped in the room, "Yes, Nya you got Daddy?"

Jay said, "I'll get him, Penny."

Penny replied, "Thanks, Jay."

Jay went into the dining room where Nya and Cornelius were waiting. Raine said, "I know you put this together Penny. It's not going to work."

She walked out the door and got in the car. Deep in thought, she knew that no matter how much love they would show each other her sisters would never approve of her new life. Deep inside, she believed they wanted her to remain a fixture in their small town like them. She wanted more and she couldn't help the way she felt.

She was suffering and things weren't perfect but she was headed to the top of her profession. All she had to do was endure for a while longer and she would be there.

But she couldn't dismiss her feelings for Jay. She did love him and she loved him more than she loved Damien. No matter how many things she did against her beliefs she wasn't going to commit adultery. She just couldn't cheat on Damien with Jay. It might feel right but it wasn't right.

***

From the moment she arrived at church everyone greeted her with so much love. It was heartwarming for Raine but she wondered if they were doing the same thing as her family, showing her love but deep inside pitying her and her lifestyle.

It was good to see Pastor Henderson. If anyone was genuine with his greeting it was him. She always believed he was a true man of God and she respected his opinion. What scared her was that he wanted to talk to her after the service. She didn't know what she was going to say to him.

Raine didn't care what everyone else thought. She was back where she started and looking better than anyone there. During the service she was called up to do a solo and Raine never batted an eye. This was her love and now she would perform one more time for her family and friends at church.

She took the stage with more confidence than she ever had. Performing in Los Angeles' best night clubs gave her a confidence that she could never have gotten at home.

She told the musicians that she was going to sing her favorite song and they all knew what that was. "Broken Pieces" could only be sung by Raine. The director of music wouldn't assign anyone else to sing that solo but Raine. No one else in the service, not even her big sister could sing the song better than she could.

She started, "In the sea of despair, I was shipwrecked and all alone, trying to find something to hold on to, I'm so lost I don't know where to turn…" Before long the crowd was revved up and into the song. It was magical from the first note. Everyone in there knew the song and knew Raine would deliver it like no other.

When it was over there wasn't a dry eye in church. Raine noticed her two sisters were crying more than anyone else. Penny came over from her place in the choir and hugged Raine. Penny said in Raine's ear, "Listen to the words you just sung."

Raine pulled back and stared at her sister. She realized that she chose to sing a song that she was secretly living…her life was in broken pieces but she wasn't prepared to accept it.

After service everyone congratulated Raine on her music contract and her performance at church. She felt like a big star in her own neighborhood. She was growing increasingly annoyed with Penny. Every chance she got she reminded Raine of Damien.

Raine was being congratulated by some of her friends when Penny came over and listened in on the conversation.

One of Raine's friends asked, "So how is married life and Hollywood?"

Raine answered, "Its great girl. Every day it gets better and better. I can't imagine doing anything else."

Penny chimed in, "That's not how I see it."

Raine paused and motioned to her friends to wait a second. She walked over to Penny and out of earshot of her friends, "If you start out here I promise you I will show out like you've never seen before."

Penny said, "You need to stop lying on church grounds."

Raine sharply responded, "Stay the…you almost made me say something that we'll both regret. Stay out of my business Penny."

She walked back over to the friends and continued laughing and talking.

After everyone was gone Raine went to Pastor Henderson's office where he was waiting. Penny sat in the outer office and waited.

Pastor Henderson said, "Girl you tore that song up, as usual. I'm so proud of you."

Raine smiled, "Thank you Pastor. I wish everyone was genuinely happy for me."

Pastor Henderson replied, "They are happy for you sweetheart but at the same time they are worried about you. We see the television reports and read the papers. We know yours is not a perfect life. We're not here to judge your decisions but we are here to comfort you when you need it."

Raine said, "My family doesn't send that message to me. They judge me every chance they get, especially my oldest sister Penny."

"As hard as it may seem to you Penny does that because she loves you so much. She can't imagine her sister suffering. If you were to close your eyes and imagine her in your situation, wouldn't you worry about her?"

Raine dropped her head. As usual Pastor Henderson knew how to touch her spirit. She began to cry. She loved Penny so much but she loved her profession and her husband. She can't make them all happy.

"Pastor, I do understand but I can't make everyone happy. I love singing and I don't want to quit. I love my husband, as well. He's not perfect but I love him. I want to get him some help, not leave him."

"Baby, I don't think Penny wants you to leave him or your profession. She just wants you to be safe. I'm not going to hold you up. I do know the Davis family loves to have Sunday dinner together in honor of Sister Diane. Just be careful my dear. It's a dangerous world we live in. You have to remember, stay prayed up!"

Raine hadn't prayed one day since she left to be in the music world. She didn't know how to respond to that statement so she lied, "I do Pastor and I will continue to pray." She felt horrible lying to him. She wished she had some marijuana in her system so she could deal with everything better.

She got up and hugged her favorite pastor. She left the room happy that she didn't have to talk about being beaten, using drugs or anything else. However, Pastor Henderson did make her think about her lack of a prayer life. She wondered if that was why she was having such a hard time. She wondered if God had forsaken her.

***

The ride from church was quiet and uneventful. The talk with Pastor Henderson didn't stop Raine from raging inside and one more thing was going to set her off. She knew that her life wasn't perfect but neither were their pitiful lives either. She thought, *'One more day Lord...just one more day and I'll be out of here. I guess I overstayed my welcome.'*

They pulled up at the house and everyone went inside. Nya cooked dinner the night before and she had already warmed it up.

Raine went into her room and kicked off her shoes. She returned to see Penny helping their father. Cornelius saw Raine and said, "Baby you tore that song up today. Your mother was proud of you. Where is she anyway?"

Raine and Penny looked at each other. Their father was getting worse mentally and Raine hated to leave him. She knew she would not see him again for months due to her tour.

She hugged her father, "Thank you daddy; I love you so much. I would do anything for you."

Penny said, "Except stay here with him."

Raine's head dropped to her arm. That was it. She took a deep breath, turned and stared at her sister, "I am sick…and tired of you. I came here to have a good time with my family and you are constantly berating me with these off hand comments."

"You're just jealous that I took a risk and it's paying off for me. I'm a successful singer and you're a pitiful nine to five worker who can't sing good enough to be on my level. I can't stand you, I can't stand it here one more minute and now I'm getting out of here!"

Nya said, "Raine, don't leave."

Raine replied, "I'm out of here, Nya. I'm out of this two bit hell-hole." Raine went to her room to grab her clothes. She didn't really think of her home as a two bit hell-hole but she was angry with her sister.

She heard Nya and Penny arguing because she was leaving. She didn't care. She was tired of pretending just to make them happy. She meant what she said and even though her life wasn't perfect, she was still a star who didn't deserve to be treated like this.

Chapter 20

Nya was angry. She was angry at Penny for forcing Raine to leave and she was angry at Raine for leaving. After dinner, she left the house and went back to the church. It was the only place she could have peace in her heart.

No one knew the pain Nya was suffering. Of all the Davis sisters she missed her mother the most. She just kept it all inside. No one even knew that she was consulting a physiatrist for her depression. She sat in the parking lot and cried.

After a while Nya got up and went inside the church. The doors were open for people to come to the altar and pray. She calmly walked to the altar and knelt before it. Her doctor couldn't help her but her God could. She needed to talk to God.

She knelt there rocking back and forth, crying. She remembered how her mother used to rock her to sleep at night. That's where she developed the habit of rocking when she was in pain. After what seemed to be an hour of praying and rocking, she felt a hand on her shoulder. She turned, "Hi Carlton, how are you doing?"

Carlton was Nya's first boyfriend. They met in high school but Carlton went off to the military and they never reconnected.

"Hi, what brings you here after service?"

Nya stood up and hugged Carlton. It had been four years since she'd seen him, "My family...it's being torn apart. My baby sister wants to be a big time singer, hell she is a big time singer now and my oldest sister aggravates her to no end. My dad had a stroke and his memory has been suffering. He keeps asking for my mom and I don't have the heart to make him relive her death again."

Carlton folded his arms, "Whoa, you have a reason to be here. Me, I was just praying for my safety. I'm headed to Iraq tomorrow."

Nya eyes opened, "Wow, I'll pray with you and for you."

The both knelt down before the altar and prayed. Nya had trouble concentrating. She still harbored feeling for Carlton. He hurt her deeply when he went off to the military but she was over that. For years she wished she had understood when he left. If she had they would have stayed together.

After the prayer Carlton asked, "Are you busy? I mean, I know your family has the weekly dinner and all but maybe we can do a movie later or something."

Nya answered, "We've had dinner and it was a fiasco. Raine stormed off back home and me and Penny…well we ain't exactly speaking. Let's go see that movie now."

They left the sanctuary and headed to the movies. Nya was happy to spend some time with her old boyfriend. He was leaving the next day but she didn't care. Maybe this day would help her to relax and not feel so depressed all the time.

Chapter 21

It was a long flight from Florida to California but Raine got to sleep for a couple of hours during the flight. The rest of the time she spent working on words for future songs and thinking about her dad. She didn't want to leave the way she did but her sister struck the last nerve possible. She was amazed how things had changed. Growing up, Nya virtually hated her and she didn't show much love for her either. Now Nya was her best friend and Penny was her nemesis.

She didn't know if Nya was just tolerating her or really happy for her but either way she wasn't judging her like Penny seemed to do. Raine and Penny were sisters and best friends growing up but now Raine couldn't stand her. Penny was still her sister and she cared about her but she was never going to go see her again.

The plane landed and Raine headed home to their condo. She wondered what kind of reception she would get from her husband after being gone for three days. She was coming home early so she guessed he would be happy. He would be ecstatic when he found out that she fought with her family and left on bad terms. He would probably throw that up in her face.

She came in the house and the driver placed her bags in the living room. No one was downstairs so she walked upstairs to change out of her church clothes and into something more comfortable.

She walked into the bedroom and was shocked, "What the hell is going on here!"

Damien jumped up out of the bed with no clothes on, "What are you doing back today? You were supposed to be coming in tomorrow."

"I can't believe you; you're sleeping with someone else! How could you? Who is this heifer, show your face!" She snatched the covers off the bed and became so angry, "LaJuan! Oh my God, I can't believe…why, you're my best friend, how could you…"

LaJuan got up, picked her clothes up off the floor and calmly walked into the bathroom.

Raine shouted, "I'm done…I'm getting a divorce."

Damien grabbed her by the shoulders and shouted in her face, "You're not going to do anything." He slapped her in the face and threw her to the ground. LaJuan came out the bathroom and said, "Be careful, you know they don't want you to damage their property before the tour."

Damien picked up his pants and took his belt off of them. He then started to beat Raine like she was his child. Raine curled up in a ball and cried. She hadn't prayed since signing her contract but she was praying now. She prayed that something would make him stop.

***

Damien was downstairs with some of his friends watching television. Raine finally got off the floor and sat on the bed. She was shivering and her body had whelps all over it but Damien managed to not hit her in the face. She held herself tightly and tried not to cry anymore. She truly believed that God had abandoned her for all she had done wrong. She wanted to leave so bad but she knew she couldn't. She felt trapped and no one there had her best interest at heart, not even LaJuan.

After a few minutes she found the strength to get up and go into the bathroom. She started the shower but then flopped to the shower floor and cried hysterically. The water ran across her beaten body causing her pain everywhere. She cried and cried, knowing no one was there for her, not even God.

***

LaJuan came in and sat down next to Raine and crossed one leg over the other. She handed Raine a drink. Raine usually didn't drink during this time of day but she didn't care anymore. She needed something to take her to another place. She needed something to make her happy again. If not happy, at least it would make her pain go away.

She poured it down her throat all in one gulp. LaJuan's eye's opened wide. She had never seen Raine drink like that before. She got Raine another drink and Raine drank it the same way.

Raine wanted to get drunk. She believed that was the only way she could handle her problems. She believed that she wasn't entitled to God's protection because she signed the contract in blood, turned on her family and starting drinking and using drugs. She planned to drink as many drinks as LaJuan would give her.

LaJuan said, "Honey, you better slow down."

Raine looked at her cross ways, "You got nerve to talk to me. You claim you hated my husband and I find you in bed with him. Then you encourage him to beat me like a child."

LaJuan replied, "Hey, this is Hollywood baby. Everybody sleeps with everybody. I was horny and so was he. You read too much into things. Besides…" She smiled seductively, "If you hadn't come back early you would've never known."

"I read too much into the fact that you're sleeping with my husband? Get away from me. You're not my friend."

LaJuan grabbed Raine sternly, "Girl, I'm the only friend you got and you better remember that." LaJuan put her finger in the middle of Raine's forehead and pushed her head back. She then slapped another drink in Raine's hand and walked out the room.

    Raine wondered if she should call home. Maybe talking to her sister would help. She thought about it some more but she wasn't sure what to do.

    She drank the last drink slower than the previous drinks. She started to feel the effects of the first two. When she was finished, she snatched all the linen off the bed, changed them and then curled up in the fetal position and fell asleep.

Chapter 22

Penny sat in her room thinking about the events from the last 24 hours. Raine had come to town and the visit started out great. Somewhere along the way, Penny couldn't control herself. She saw the bruises on her baby sister and she couldn't contain herself any longer.

She loved her baby sister so much and the thought of someone beating on her bothered her to no end. Nya didn't want to face it because she didn't want Raine to leave but Penny told Nya that's not the way to handle it. They obviously had different opinions.

Penny believed they had to convince Raine to leave that life and come back home. If not the life then she needed to leave Damien for sure. She felt the devil had her in his grasp and he was going to destroy Raine.

Penny's next opportunity would be in three months when Raine came back home for her concert. She planned to go to her hotel, sit her down and have a good long talk with her sister. She would do it calmly so she wouldn't get Raine upset.

The ringing of the house phone broke Penny's concentration. Penny answered the phone, "Hello." There was no response but Penny could hear someone breathing. She asked again, "Hello…Raine is that you?"

No answer but this time Penny swore she could hear crying. She called out on the phone, "Raine, baby what's wrong; Raine…Raine!"

The phone went dead. Penny didn't know what to do. Something made her sister call but she didn't answer. She heard her dad in the living room and went out to see what he needed. Cornelius asked, "Who was it baby?"

Penny answered, "No one answered. I think it might have been Raine. I could hear breathing but she wouldn't answer."

Cornelius smiled, "Where's my baby, tell her to come see me."

Penny nodded, "Okay Daddy, I'll tell her but first you need to lie down and take a nap. You need to get some rest."

Chapter 23

Penny sat down in the law office of Jacob Percy. It had been a few years since she sat in his office but it looked much the same. He was clean and neat, nothing was out of place. His degrees and certificates lined the walls. She knew he had to be a great lawyer but most of all he was a great family friend. If he wasn't, there was no way her parents could have afforded him.

The last time she sat in his office was to have both her parent's 'Last Will and Testaments' done. This time she had to sign a Power of Attorney to take responsibility for all of her ailing father's legal matters.

It wasn't something she relished in doing because it meant her father wasn't capable of caring for himself any longer. Acceptance of this fact was hard on both her and Nya but the doctor's convinced them it needed to be done.

With his ongoing medical issues it was necessary for someone to take control. Penny felt the pressure of taking care of the Davis family but she couldn't allow it to break her spirit. No matter how down she got, she knew she had to stand on her faith in the Lord.

As they finished up all the papers, Penny asked, "Mr. Percy do you think there is a way to get Raine out of that music contract?"

Mr. Percy replied, "There's always a way to get out of any contract if you have enough money to pay a lawyer." He chuckled, "But then again if the other side doesn't want to let her go then they're going to pay lawyers to fight it."

"I see."

"Your sisters best bet would have been to have a lawyer read her contract before she signed it. Then she would have had some advice on what she could or could not do now."

"My sister is so head strong Mr. Percy; she didn't think anyone could tell her anything. I don't even know if she wants out of the contract. I'm just asking for my own edification."

Mr. Percy nodded his head, "Well that's your first problem. If she doesn't want out of the contract, then there's nothing you can do but pray for her. I've been a lawyer for 40 years and a Christian for virtually all of them. I've seen many people sign contracts that weren't good for them but the music industry…well that's one industry that you have to be very careful what you sign. Remember Lucifer was involved in music in Heaven so it's no wonder he would be involved in it on Earth."

Penny looked down to the floor, "Yes sir, I do remember hearing that he was the director of music in Heaven."

Mr. Percy leaned back in his chair, "No, no baby. That's a common misconception. The Bible doesn't say that Satan was the director or minister of music. What is says is, he was made of tabrets and pipes. It doesn't say he was in charge of the music."

Penny smiled as she realized that she just learned something, "I didn't know that; thanks."

Mr. Percy thumbed through his Bible, "Yes here it is in Ezekiel 28:13. It says, 'the workmanship of thy tabrets and of thy pipes was prepared in thee in the day that that thou wast created.' He was made with the ability to play music, not placed in charge of it."

Penny asked, "What are tabrets?"

Mr. Percy answered, "They are small one sided drums; we call them tambourines today."

"Thanks Mr. Percy. What can I do about my sister? It just pains me that she is suffering but doesn't want anyone to know it. She wants everyone to think she's living the life when I know she's not happy."

"Pray…there's nothing you can do until your sister decides she wants out. Come on, where two or more are gathered in His name, He will be here too. Let's pray for her."

***

Penny sat across from Jaden at dinner. It was nice to be out with her man and try to forget about the problems with the Davis family. Her dad was slowly deteriorating in front of them and Raine was suffering inside and didn't want help.

Since her mom was gone the family problems all fell on her now. She had to be the mom, the sister and the daughter. Jaden took her hand and slowly rubbed it. It felt good. She smiled without looking up. That loving chill ran up and down her spine.

She said, "You seem to always know what to do, don't you?"

Jaden smiled back, "Because I watch and I feel whatever my queen is feeling. If you hurt, so do I. If you're happy, so am I. That's love, baby."

"Yes, it is sweetheart. Raine said she wanted to be at the wedding. I guess we should set the date for after her tour is over, so she can be there. Who knows if she still wants to be there or not."

Jaden said, "We can make it for any day you wish baby. It's your day and I'm there to serve you."

Penny smiled. She loved him so much. He was the only thing in her life that was constant. She had no issues with her man.

Jaden switched his seat to the one next to Penny, "Now, I want you to forget about all of your issues and focus on the wedding."

Penny said, "Honey, I don't think Raine wants to be in it or attend anymore. She stormed out of here like she wasn't ever planning on returning. It hurts my heart so badly. I just can't help it. I say things when I'm around her but it's because I love her, not because I want to hurt her. She just doesn't get it."

"You just said we should schedule it for a date after her tour," said Jaden. Let's just stick to that and if she comes, she comes. If not, we still get married. But didn't she call last night?"

"I think it was her, I can't be sure." She laid her head on Jaden's shoulder, "I wish I could help. I really do want to help her."

Jaden sipped on his wine, "Well, when she wants to be helped, I'm sure you will be there."

She kissed him on the cheek. He was right. She would be there in a minute for her sister no matter what transpired between them. She was that way about both her sisters and her father. Even with Nya not speaking to her she would still be by her side in a minute if she needed it. Nothing could break her bond with them.

***

Penny woke the next morning in the arms of the man she loved and planned to marry. She felt at peace lying on his chest like it was made just for her. Her phone startled her, "Hello."

"Penny…you need to come to the hospital quick!" It was Nya and she was crying.

Penny jumped up, "What happened?"

"It's Daddy; he had another stroke. I'm on my way with him to the hospital."

"I'll be there in a minute." She thought as she struggled to get dressed, *'Oh my God, please don't let my daddy die…please!'*

The commotion woke Jaden, "What's wrong, baby?"

"It's Daddy." Penny said, "He had another stroke. I have to get to the hospital. Oh my goodness, I should have been there last night; Daddy…"

Jaden grabbed her by the shoulders, "Penny…you can't do it all. Your presence wouldn't have changed anything. The best you can do is get to the hospital and be there for him now."

Penny tried to calm down. She knew he was right, "Will you come with me."

"Are you kidding me? Where the heck else do you think I'm going?"

Penny smiled inside. No matter what she was going through, her man was by her side. She needed him and he never let her down. The both quickly got dressed and rushed to the hospital.

***

Penny and Jaden ran into the hospital. They found Nya standing in the hallway, "Nya what's going on, what are they saying?"

Through her tears Nya answered, "Nothing right now. They're working on him and said they will come out when they're done; all we can do is wait."

Penny folded her arms and dropped her head, "I can't believe this is happening. It's only been a year since mom and now dad. What are we gonna do, Nya?"

Nya hugged her and Jaden joined them. Nya said, "All we can do is pray for him. He's all we got and God knows it."

Nya looked Penny in the eyes, "Penny, big sis, I'm sorry for the things I said Sunday after Raine left. I should have been more considerate of your opinion."

Penny hugged her tightly, "Don't worry Nya. I should have held back my comments. We would have had at least one more day with our sister. Me and my big mouth, huh?"

Nya laughed, "Yeah."

Penny moved over to Jaden and laid her head on his shoulder.

Penny asked Nya, "Did you try to call Raine?"

"No…what good would it do? She won't come back, she didn't the last time so why would she this time."

Jaden added, "Someone should call her. If she decides not to come back than that's her choice but at least tell her what's going on."

Penny looked at Jaden then Nya, "You should call. She might be more prone to take a call from you than me."

Nya replied, "Okay, I'll call." She pulled out her phone while Penny and Jaden watched.

The phone rang but there was no answer. Nya left a message for her sister so she would know about their father.

***

It had been three hours since the ambulance brought their father to the hospital. More family had arrived but Penny managed to stay in a quiet corner by herself. Jaden went to get her some coffee but she wasn't even sure she would drink it when he returned.

The doctor finally came out of the room. Penny and Nya both ran to him. The doctor removed his glasses and wiped the sweat from his brow, "Ladies which one of you is Penelope Davis?"

Penny answered, "I am…I go by Penny."

"Okay Penny, as you know your father suffered another stroke. He's going to be paralyzed. Now you have to remember paralysis is one of the most common disabilities resulting from stroke. Your dad has lost the use of his muscles on the left side of his body. This happened because there are problems in the messages between the muscles and brain. He's going to need daily care."

Penny and Nya held their hands over their mouth. Penny leaned against the wall and reached for her sister's hand. Nya took it and squeezed it tightly. They both were worried.

Their world was caving in on them and Penny as the oldest had to try and hold on. She had to try and keep the Davis family from completely falling apart.

The doctor asked, "Will there be someone at home to watch him at all times?"

Penny didn't even hear the question. Nya pushed her on the shoulder to get her attention.

"Huh? I'm sorry, I wasn't paying attention."

Nya sighed, "Yes doctor, me and my sister will work it out and someone will be at the house to watch our father."

The doctor looked at each of them. He touched Penny on the shoulder, "It's going to be alright. It's a difficult adjustment for a family but be thankful that you still have your father. A lot people don't survive this."

He smiled at Penny and somehow it made her feel better. Jaden put his arm around her and held her close to him. Nya told the rest of the family what was going on.

No one heard from Raine. Penny wanted to believe that she just hadn't gotten the message but part of her felt she just didn't call back.

Chapter 24

Raine woke up feeling horrible. She had hangovers before but this one was different. She felt like she had something stronger, something that knocked her on her behind and it wasn't the alcohol. She remembered drinking a lot. Damien gave her drinks until she was so intoxicated that she didn't fully realize what was happening. She slept the entire morning away and didn't realize how she got to her bed.

She looked at her naked body and realized quickly that she had sex the night before. She didn't know who with but she had it with someone. She could only pray that it was her husband. She didn't think he would have allowed anyone else to touch her.

Downstairs she heard voices. One of them was Damien and he was arguing with someone. She put on her bathrobe and peeked out the bedroom door. From her advantage point she could see Damien from behind. There were three men in suits downstairs and Damien was pleading his case saying, "I had nothing to do with it!"

One of the men took Damien by the arm and slammed his hand on the coffee table. His fingers were spread out on the table and the leader slammed a hammer on one of Damien's fingers.

Raine gasped and eased the door closed. Fear took up residence in her body and she rushed to the bathroom and puked. If those men would do that to Damien they would kill her easily.

When she came out she heard the front door close. She peeked out again and Damien was on his knees in pain. She saw LaJuan come over to Damien, put her arm around him to console him.

She came out the room and stood at the top of the stairs and looked down at them. LaJuan saw her, "It's not what you think, Raine."

Raine went back in the bedroom and sat on the bed. She didn't like the things Damien did to her but what did he do to deserve that? A few minutes later, Damien came in the bedroom with a towel wrapped around his hand.

He said, "I have to go to the hospital. I'll be back in a few."

"Damien, what happened? What was that all about?"

"I can't talk to you about it." He looked sternly at her, "Just stay out of it Raine and if I were you…" He moved closer to her and whispered, "I wouldn't trust LaJuan."

Raine was confused. On one hand Damien abused her and on the other he tries to protect her. She didn't know what to think. Everything was turning upside down.

Now she was really worried about her sexual exploits the night before. Was it with Damien or not? After seeing what she saw she had to ask him. She prayed that it was her husband and not someone else. She asked, "Damien, did we have sex last night?"

He looked confused, "Of course we did. You don't remember?"

"I must have drunk too much. I don't remember much of anything."

Damien said, "We'll talk later." He went out the bedroom and left Raine standing there. She looked out the bedroom door and LaJuan was sitting on the couch. She raised her glass toward Raine. Raine just walked away to get dressed.

***

Raine went through a grueling rehearsal for her upcoming tour. This practice was worse than any of the previous rehearsals. Everything had to be timed out and sharp, no mistakes.

Damien came back from the hospital halfway through the rehearsal and made them stay even longer. It was after ten o' clock in the evening when they finally stopped.

Raine was tired and hungry when Damien came over to her, "Hey baby. You okay? Sorry about all this but we need to have it right."

Sometimes he could be an angel and others he was Satan himself. Raine answered, "You working a sister. I don't know about giving you some tonight."

They both laughed. Raine thought she might get slapped for the comment but Damien seemed a little calmer tonight. She deduced it might have come from the events from the morning.

Damien eased up to Raine, "Well we're going to see if you can relax some so I can get some. I never get enough of my wife."

Raine smirked. She wanted to remind him of his illicit affair with her so called best friend but she didn't want to ruin the moment. She said, "Well if you feed me, maybe, just maybe, I can see my way to changing my mind." She dropped her head to the side doing her best sexy look.

Damien replied, "Well, we gettin' you some food baby; oh yeah!"

Raine asked, "How's your finger?"

"It'll be okay." The two of them laughed and walked arm in arm out the rehearsal hall to get some food.

On the ride over to the restaurant Raine looked at her phone. She had a missed call from Nya. She said, "Oh Nya called me this morning. Wow, I'm slacking on checking my phone."

Damien said, "I thought you were through with your family?"

"I said she called me baby, not me calling her. Oh she left a message, let's see what she said. She probably begging me to come back home again. They're so jealous of me."

"They have a right to be, you're the best, baby."

"Awwww…" Raine listened to the message and sat up in her seat. She said, "Oh my God, my daddy."

Damien looked at her, "What, what's going on?"

"My daddy had another stroke."

Damien didn't say anything. Raine got quiet. She couldn't eat now because she was worried about her father. She had to call Nya back. She looked at Damien, "I have to call back. I have to know about my daddy."

"Go ahead baby; do what you gotta do."

Raine was happy to hear that. She was thankful that he didn't stop her from calling. Maybe she would give him some if everything was okay with her dad.

Raine dialed the number and waited for Nya to answer. It was one in the morning in Florida but all she could do was hope that Nya was still up. After a few rings she answered, "Raine?"

"Hey girl, how's Daddy?"

"What took you so long to call back?"

"I'm sorry but I've been rehearsing and I just didn't get to my phone until now. How's my daddy?"

"He's okay but he's paralyzed on his left side. Someone is going to have to be with him all day; me and Penny have arranged a schedule. It's gonna be tough on us but with Auntie Rose and Aunt Bea helping, we think we can do it."

Raine started to cry. She said, "Nya I can send some money to help out. We can hire a nurse to free you guys up."

"You know Penny would never take it. She took those clothes but that was before she saw the bruises."

Raine sternly shouted, "Then don't tell her behind. I'll send it to you and you hire a nurse. It's our father too and she shouldn't get all the say in this."

"Okay, I'll text you my bank account information; thanks Raine."

"No Nya, thank you for seeing past everything and letting me help"

Nya responded, "I love you, baby girl."

That was the first time Nya called Raine "baby girl" and to add to it, Nya told her she loved her. That statement brought a smile to Raine's face. All these years Nya refused to call her baby girl but now she did.

"I love you too Nya. Please keep me informed on everything. I know I can count on you."

"Raine, Penny wanted to call you too but she didn't think you would take her call."

"She's probably right; take care, girl."

"You too, baby girl."

Raine hung up the phone and looked at Damien. They pulled up to the restaurant. She said, "He's going to be alright but he's paralyzed on the left side."

Damien replied, "Sorry to hear that. At least you can send money to help them out. You see if you hadn't signed this deal where would they be now?"

"True, but you can't make Penny see that for nothing."

They both walked inside the restaurant and sat down to eat. Raine's mind was on her daddy but she was glad his life was not threatened.

***

Raine and Damien sat quietly in their condo drinking. Raine found it easier and easier to drink now and she developed a taste for mojitos. She enjoyed mojitos mostly because of the sugar. She didn't really care for the rum but the sugar, lemon juice, mint and club soda hid the taste of the rum enough for her to enjoy it.

Before she met Damien she never drank any alcohol. Now, she had gotten to the point where she needed it every day and enjoyed it.

Raine said, "Oh Damien, I'm so weak and tired. You worked me too much today. I can hardly keep my eyes open."

Damien replied, "Well, I have something that will give you some energy. You had a taste last night but I'm betting you don't remember."

"What, five hour energy, red bull, give me some baby?"

"Naw baby, this is better than either of those."

Raine saw him light a flame under a tube of something. She said, "What is that?"

Damien answered, "Crack, the good stuff."

Raine was shocked, "What?"

Damien nodded his head, "Yeah, you gonna love this."

"Damien, I don't know about drugs sweetie. Didn't you say Elaine got strung out on drugs?"

Damien smiled, "Yeah, but you can handle it. She was weak and useless. Plus, you handled it easily last night." He moved beside her, "Hey haven't I delivered on everything I told you. I told you you'd be a star and you are. I told you have a bestselling single and CD, your single is number one and the CD is going to be number one. Now you're going to have a major tour, unheard of for a first time artist. Trust me, you'll love this."

He put the pipe in his mouth and inhaled. His eyes went to the back of his head as he appeared to enjoy it. He handed the pipe to Raine and she took it. She was scared and nervous.

Damien said, "Just put it in your mouth and inhale it."

She inhaled and started coughing and patting her chest, "Oh my…that mess is strong!"

Damien laughed as he took another hit. Raine took more. As the night went on it became easier and easier for her to take a hit. The effects were beginning to overwhelm her as she started seeing the room slowly begin to spin. It felt good. She no longer thought about any of her problems or concerns. Instead all she thought about was the high.

***

Raine woke up in the same condition as she did the previous day but this time she remembered the crack cocaine she ingested. She smiled and looked for Damien. She couldn't remember having two good nights in a row with her husband. Maybe things were changing for the better.

She looked out the bedroom and Damien was on the phone. She smiled at him and he waved at her. She decided to get dressed. Rehearsal time would be there soon and she wanted to be well rested.

In the bathroom she smiled in the mirror. Her bruises were gone but a couple of whelps were still there. She reasoned that soon they would be gone as well. At least she didn't have any more broken bones.

Life was good right now. She remembered that her father was paralyzed but she would send some money to help her sisters hire a nurse.

She slowly got showered and dressed. When she came downstairs she realized that Damien was already dressed and watching television. He had one arm on the back of the couch and the other in his lap. He was looking like the world was his oyster.

She asked, "How long you been up?"

"Baby it's one in the afternoon. You don't know how to hold your crack."

They both laughed. Then Raine realized what Damien said and she stopped cold, "What; it's that late?"

"Yeah, you were obviously so out of it that it took you that long to sleep it off." He laughed again. She joined in with him, realizing that they were still having a great time together. For the first time since her marriage she was truly happy. She didn't consider herself truly in love but she loved these moments. There just weren't enough of them. She said, "I guess not. I need something to eat."

She went into the kitchen and made them some lunch. Life was truly good for her now. She made it through the tough part and now she can be happy.

Chapter 25

Damien was watching rehearsal and barking out commands to the group. He wanted Raine's performance to be the best ever seen in the industry. She was going to be opening for some big acts so he was being as tough as he could on her and the group.

Don walked up to him and stood beside him. Damien said, "Raine wants to send money to her family. She wants them to get a nurse to care for her father."

Don replied without looking at him, "Okay, I'll see to it."

Damien turned and put his hand on Don's shoulder, "No. Make sure something comes up and the paperwork is lost. I don't want her throwing her money away on them. They didn't want this life for her so let them suffer and pay for it themselves."

"You cold man but you're my boy so, I got 'cha. What if she asks about it?"

Damien answered, "Tell her you put the paperwork in and you'll check on it. Then fix some paperwork up and show her that it's in the system. She'll be too busy on tour to ask any more questions."

Don nodded. Damien continued, "Yeah, she's loving life right now but she doesn't realize that the crack is starting to consume her. She wanted more and more last night. In a week she'll want me and only me because I can provide it to her. Then, I'll cut her off from her family all together. This money thing will help add to that. When they see Raine isn't sending any money they'll be mad at her and stop trying to call her. My plan is working just like I want it to."

Don smiled, "But didn't that get you in trouble with the suits and Elaine?"

"This time we'll be more careful. This time we need to make sure it can't be traced back to me."

"Right, I'll take care of my end."

Damien said, "Oh and don't trust LaJuan. I found out she works for them. She has all along. They hired her to get close to Raine and get information as to what was going on. She was the one that told them about Elaine. They couldn't prove I killed her but they believe I did. That's why my finger is in this sling. They said next time I'll lose it."

"Wow dude. You're lucky that's all they did."

"Yeah, they know they need me to find talent for them. Raine won't last forever and they'll want new talent."

"True… later, bro."

Damien continued to look on and follow the rehearsal. Raine was beautiful and her singing was better than anyone Damien had ever recruited. He knew audiences all across the county would love her performance. She didn't need any electronic enhances, she was a natural. He just wanted to make as much money as he could from her then drop her for another cash cow. He had no love for her at all.

Chapter 26

Penny fed her father his lunch. It was a daily task that she had come to enjoy. Her father could hardly talk and totally depended on Penny and Nya but they both enjoyed caring for him. When they were children both their parents cared for their every need. Now it was payback time.

She remembered doing the same for her mother before she passed away. The three years her mother battled cancer was tough on all of them but Penny wouldn't leave her mother's side then and she won't leave her father now.

Cornelius had given them everything in their lives and they had no problem taking care of him now. Both of them knew Raine's absence was killing their father.

Penny frowned when she thought of the promise Raine made to send money to Nya but Nya had not received anything. The news stories coming out of her camp told of Raine drinking, smoking and doing drugs. Penny couldn't believe her baby sister would turn to such a life but she had. Pastor Henderson was right; she needed to be surrounded by likeminded people.

The newspaper sat on a table next to her and it had Raine's picture on the front. She was smoking a cigar and partying in a nightclub. The article's title was 'Good Girl Gone Bad?' It told the story of Raine getting into a brawl with another woman at the club over Damien. Penny shook her head as she moved the paper away from her father's view.

In a few days Raine would be in town for her concert. Penny didn't know if she would come see the family or not but she needed to go see her at her hotel. She needed to tell her that her father wanted to see her.

Nya walked in the living room, "Hey Penny, I'll be there to take over in one minute okay."

"Don't rush girl, I have nothing to do. Jaden has to work tonight."

"Sweet, then we can hang out together. We haven't done that in a long time."

Penny smiled, "Yeah, let's pop in a movie and get wild." They both laughed.

Nya said, "Like your sister?"

Penny laughed, "That's not exactly what I meant."

Nya asked, "So, you think she'll come this weekend?"

"No, but I'm going to the hotel and see if they will let me in to see her behind."

Nya replied, "Well, it doesn't hurt to try. I'm pissed at her because she claimed she wanted to help us by sending money and she didn't even do it. She just turned completely against her family. She hasn't even called in months."

Penny wiped her dad's mouth and stood up, "Yeah, I know but that's what happens when you become so consumed with the world. She's forgotten everything and everybody who truly cares for her. Pastor Henderson warned me of that."

"Of what?"

"That if you don't surround yourself with people who believe as you believe you could become consumed by their world; he didn't say it exactly like that but that's what he meant."

Nya said, "Well all we can do is keep doing what we're doing. I'm sad because of Daddy's condition but like the doctor said, 'at least he's still alive'."

"Amen to that, my sister."

***

Penny was in the grocery store getting food for dinner when someone tapped her on her shoulder. She quickly turned around, "Jay, how are you? I heard you graduated and got drafted by some team out west."

"Hey Penny; I did and yes I was picked up late in the second round by Portland. My chances of making the team aren't good but hey, I have to give it my best. If it doesn't work out, I still have a job with Corinthians."

Penny smiled and poked him in the chest, "You got God on your side so your chances are better than you may know."

"Thanks Penny, I appreciate that. Have you heard from Raine?"

Penny nodded her head, "Nope. She doesn't call and she won't return our calls. I don't even listen to the news anymore because I'm tired of hearing about the things she's involved in now. Since she's from here and her concert is approaching they have something on the news every night. It's embarrassing at some of the things I see and hear. I only wish she would listen to someone."

Jay nodded his head, "Yeah, that fight in the club was embarrassing. They say she was so high she didn't even remember where she was that night." He looked down.

Penny tried to console him, "It's unbelievable Jay; that just isn't the Raine I know and have known for all of her life. She isn't the one you knew either. Damien got his hands on her and turned her into something none of us recognize. But, I do believe she still loves you and I believe that love will find it's way to the surface and she'll regain her senses. Hang in there Jay."

She knew Jay still loved Raine. It was written all over his face. She liked Jay from the moment Raine brought him home. She knew that the two of them could have lasted forever. If Raine had stayed and finished her degree, they would be getting married now.

Jay agreed, "Yeah, that Damien guy turned my baby out. If I could just talk to her, maybe she would listen."

Penny put her hand on his shoulder, "Well, I'm going to that hotel tomorrow. I hope she'll see me. You should come with me. Maybe she'll see us both."

Jay said excitedly, "Cool, I will. I'll come over to the Davis house and pick you up."

Penny laughed, "The Davis house…people still say that? Okay I'll be ready and prayed up."

"Bye Penny and thanks."

"Bye Jay and you're welcome. I just hope it works."

202

Chapter 27

As she walked the streets of the downtown Los Angeles, heads turned everywhere. She was easily considered the best looking woman on any street. Her tight black mini skirt hugged her body like it was made solely for her. It was accented by the genuine black leather booties on her feet.

Her blouse was a royal blue and specifically tailored to show just enough cleavage to make men lust to see more. She was desirable by everyone she came in contact with.

LaJuan entered the small diner on the corner and eased into one of the booth seats. Across from her was someone who she knew wanted her badly. He could never get enough of her and would do whatever LaJuan wanted him to do.

Her beauty coupled with her English accent excited men everywhere. She asked, "So why did you tell me to meet you here?"

Don answered, "Damien got Raine hooked on crack."

"I know that. She'll still perform better than anyone on the planet right now so I don't care what she does as long as she's able to sell tickets and get people to buy her CD."

Don said, "I know, but I thought you should know in case it becomes an issue later."

"What concerns me Don is that you didn't tell me this earlier. I had to find out from someone else." She lit up a cigarette and shook her head. Her hair fell back into place with ease, "I'm beginning to wonder if I can trust you."

Don's mouth was wide open, "You can trust me LaJuan, I promise. He also knows you work for the suits. I'll tell you all I know, I promise."

LaJuan threw her head back and to one side, "Really. I guess we're going to have to see about that because I'm just not feeling you anymore. I use to want you so much but now, I just don't know."

"Noooo don't break up with me LaJuan, please!"

LaJuan shook her head slowly from side to side, "I'll think about it but in the meantime I'd better see some results; you feel me?"

Don grabbed her hands, "Yes, you'll see some results. Trust me I'll tell you everything when it happens; I promise."

LaJuan got up and kissed him on the cheek. She had total control over him and she knew it. She gave him just enough sex to make him want her so much that he couldn't stand to lose her. She had a power that he couldn't break from even if he tried.

LaJuan turned and walked out of the diner. Every head watched her hips sway from side to side as she left. She paused at the door giving Don a little more to look at in case he had ideas of betraying her.

Chapter 28

Raine's entourage reached her hometown. She rode into town in a limo from the airport headed to her hotel. In one hand, she had a glass of Champaign and in the other hand was a crack cocaine pipe. She was drunk and high.

"Woo hoo…here I am, back home to turn up! I'm gonna leave this city in flames, cause I'm soooooo hot!"

Damien had his arm around her, "Tell 'em, baby. Nobody has anything on my woman."

"That's right Damien, you tell 'em. Your wife is pretty, fine, sexy and can sing anybody under the table. Woo hoo!"

Damien said, "Hey everybody raise your glass and let's make a toast to the number one CD in the country…'Let it Raine' by my baby, Raine!"

Everyone in the limo raised their glasses and made a toast to Raine's hit CD. The CD had been downloaded more times than any CD in Fresh City history. She was clearly the number one sensation and the best thing ever put out on the Fresh City label. She was on top of the world and no one could tell her otherwise.

Raine asked, "Hey driver open the roof." The driver complied and the roof of the limo slowly opened. Raine stood up and put her head and shoulders outside the limo.

She heard everyone in the limo laughing and enjoying themselves. They were egging her on to do something crazy. Raine had become the entertainer on and off stage.

As the limo passed people on the street she waved and screamed at them and the people were excited to see Raine. She saw her old boyfriend, the one before Jay and blew him a kiss. She shouted, "Hey Charles, I miss you baby!"

Charles responded, "I miss you, sweetheart."

Raine was so high she didn't know the mistake she was making, "Come see me at the Hilton, honey!"

Before Charles could answer Damien yanked her back in the limo. Raine sternly asked, "Why did you do that?"

Damien quickly shouted, "You're embarrassing me!" Everyone in the limo suddenly got quiet. One of the musicians said, "Come on man, she's just playing around and having some fun with her fans." Damien stared coldly at him.

Raine added, "I'm not embarrassing you. I'm just having some fun like TJ said." She stood back up and started yelling to people on the street again.

The limo finally pulled into the hotel and Raine was still giggling and having a great time. The noise level returned and everyone in the limo started having a great time again. That is everyone except Damien. He wasn't enjoying it at all.

They got out the limo and headed to the penthouse room. Raine paraded through the lobby yelling at everyone. She was shouting, "Let it Raine!" Half of her Champaign spilled on the ground before she got in the evaluator.

Raine went into the penthouse and went directly to the bar in the room. She noticed Damien talking to the security guards and then he closed the door.

Raine walked over to him with a drink in each hand. She handed one of the drinks to Damien but he slapped it out of her hand and punched her in the face.

The blow knocked her backwards and to the ground where her head hit the floor. She was dazed. Damien pounced on top of her and slapped her several times across the face.

"Next time I tell you to stop embarrassing me, you better listen!"

Raine was groggy and trying to cover her face, "Please Damien, stop! Don't hit me anymore." She continued to plead with him until she heard a strong and powerful voice from the door, "Damien!"

The slaps stop. Raine laid there holding her face scared to look out. Damien got up and walked out the door. Her party and fun was over and misery was back. She was humiliated again by this man who was her husband. Nothing she ever did pleased him. Even in her hometown she couldn't have fun, she couldn't enjoy herself or her life.

She got up and ran into one of the private bedrooms and locked the door. She was tired of being a punching bag. She thought she had gotten past all of that but she realized she would never get past it. He would never stop beating her.

***

She didn't know what to do. She was in her hometown and could easily get to her family but she wanted to finish the tour. Music was her life and she had a contract. She didn't need Damien to sing. She rationalized that she would finish the tour then leave Damien.

Raine's drug and alcohol induced state caused her to drift off to sleep. She woke up to the sounds of someone pounding on her room door. Damien was shouting her name and demanding that she open the door. She was afraid to do it.

He finally kicked in the door. Raine screamed and tried to run into the bathroom but Damien grabbed her by the waist before she could. He was much stronger than she was. He put both hands on her shoulders and held her tightly, "You need to get it together. You have a press conference in an hour." He shook her vigorously then he pushed her down on the bed and coldly stared at her lying there. She hated him. No matter how much she tried to love him she couldn't. She slowly got up and went to get her suitcase.

She dragged her suitcase to another room, locked the door and cried. For the first time in months she hated her life. The success she enjoyed wasn't enough for the misery she was suffering in her personal life. In a way, she knew Penny was right. The price had been too high. She was a drunk, a drug addict and victim of abuse. She had to get away from Damien.

In her room she fell to her knees in front of her suitcase and cried more and more. She called out, "Penny, please help me." She opened her suitcase and saw a pouch where Damien hid some of the crack cocaine. She thought, *'That bastard hid it in my suitcase so I could get caught. I hate him!'*

She took the drugs and cooked it…all of it. Then she put it into a syringe and injected it into her arm.

The effect was immediate. She fell to the floor and everything spun. She saw her life racing by…she saw the end.

***

She didn't know how long it had been but Raine slowly opened her eyes to see her big sister and ex-boyfriend standing by her hospital bed. She was still groggy but she knew this meeting wasn't going to be good. She knew Penny would put her down sarcastically. She said to herself, *'This is just what I need.'*

She asked, "Where am I?"

Penny slowly answered, "You're in the hospital…Bay Memorial. Damien made it so no one would know that you're here but the family."

Raine looked down. She didn't know what to say to Penny and she certainly couldn't look at or say anything to Jay.

Penny continued, "Why Raine? Why did you do it? Don't you know that you have family who loves you? It doesn't matter what we have gone through, you are still my sister. Nothing can change that…nothing."

Raine continued to look down. Jay touched her hand softly. She quickly moved it back because she didn't feel worthy. The tears eased down her cheek.

Raine was embarrassed by her actions and couldn't bring herself to look either of them in the eyes.

Jay reached down and hugged her. She couldn't hug him back. It felt good to feel his touch again. She loved him and she knew it. Jay was the one she should have married. She looked at Penny for the first time and then closed her eyes. Jay kissed her lightly on the lips.

Damien shouted, "What's going on here? You're kissing my wife?"

Jay stepped back from Raine. Penny said, "Don't you start in here. My sisters trying to recover and the last thing she needs is you acting like a jerk. Unlike you, we happen to care about her!"

Raine grabbed her arm, "Penny, don't…"

Damien pointed at Penny and turned to walk away.

Raine said, "You should've done that. Now I'll have to pay for it."

Penny replied, "No, you won't. Raine, I don't care if you're a million selling artist or not, you're my sister and you don't deserve to be treated like this. I don't care if you end up hating me but I'm going to put an end to this mess."

She walked out the room and Raine tried to sit up. Jay stopped her, "Wait Raine you can't get up so quick."

The doctor came in the room, "Where do you think you're going young lady?"

Raine answered, "I need to help my sister."

The doctor said, "I'm sorry but you're not going anywhere. We need to keep you under observation for a few days. We also need to determine if this was deliberate or not."

Raine eased by down on the bed, "I can't stay here for a few days. I have a concert tomorrow night and several events today and tomorrow."

The doctor replied, "You won't be attending any of those."

"I beg to differ. I've been waiting to play my hometown all this time and I'm not going to let this stop me." She looked at Jay, "Can you get Damien for me, please?"

Jay went into the hallway and after a couple of minutes he returned with Damien and Penny.

Raine shouted, "Damien, this doctor is saying I have to stay here and miss all the events and the concert."

Damien replied, "Don't worry the record company is taking care of everything. You won't miss anything."

The doctor rolled his eyes at Damien. Penny jumped in the conversation, "Wait a minute, if the doctor says she needs to stay then she needs to stay."

Raine said, "Stay out of it Penny, please. I need to do this. I need to play my hometown, if I don't do anything else in this life, I need to play my hometown. I know you don't believe in me or my decisions but for once out of love for me; please stay out of this."

Penny walked out of the room and Raine dropped her head, "I can never please her."

Jay said, "Let me talk to her." Jay walked out after Penny.

Damien asked, "Who is that idiot?"

Raine answered, "My ex-boyfriend and he's not an idiot. He just loves me."

"And you still love him?"

The doctor said, "Okay, everything looks okay but I'm still standing firm on my opinion that you need to stay under observation. Until someone overrules me, you're staying here, young lady."

Raine looked at Damien. He said, "Don't worry. Get some rest and I'll have you out in a couple of minutes."

The doctor rolled his eyes at Damien again and walked out. Damien said, "You never answered my question."

Raine paused and then answered, "I don't love him anymore." That was a lie but it got Damien out of the room. She laid her head back on the pillow and sighed. She thought about all the things that happened to her since she met Damien. Most of them she hated but the one thing she had was, her success. If she could get rid of Damien, she could have a happy life.

Being in the hospital room wasn't all bad for Raine. She felt a sense of calm come over her and she drifted off to sleep.

Two hours later Damien woke Raine up from her sleep. She asked, "Am I being released?" The nurse came in with papers for Raine.

The nurse said, "Here are your release papers. I need you to read them and sign at the bottom."

Raine looked up at Damien. He was smiling at her, pleased at getting her released.

Raine signed the papers and Damien helped her get out of the bed. He retrieved her clothes and handed them to her.

Damien said, "Get dressed; we have just enough time for you to go back to the hotel, change and make it to the radio station for your interview."

Raine said, "Okay." She looked up, trying to say she wanted him to leave the room.

Damien replied, "I guess you want me to step out."

She smiled, "Please."

Damien left the room and Raine got dressed. They headed back to the hotel and she started her day.

Chapter 29

Penny sat at the dinner table with Nya and Jaden. As with most of the dinner time discussion over the last few months, the main topic surrounded Raine. Penny said, "She clearly doesn't want to be with that jerk anymore. I saw the look in her eye when Jay hugged her. I know she'd rather be with him than Damien."

Nya asked, "You think she tried to kill herself?"

"I know it. It was obvious to me. She was ashamed…you know how Raine looks when she's embarrassed about something."

Nya managed a smile, "I do, but she's changed so much that I didn't think any of the signs would be there anymore."

Jaden said, "You know this is the time that Raine has waited for all her life. Maybe she wants to do this concert and then leave Damien. I'm just saying…maybe there's a chance."

Penny replied, "You might be right Jaden but I don't see it. She's somehow hypnotized by that man. I saw more fresh bruises on her body so he's still beating her behind."

Nya responded, "My God, I never envisioned this happening to any Davis woman. We just don't play that mess. At least I thought we didn't"

Penny said, "Well, she wanted to be on the big stage and she clearly was willing to do anything or allow anything to get there. I think she won't leave him because in her mind it would be an admission that she was wrong. She'd rather be miserable than admit that." They all nodded in agreement. Penny pointed at Jaden, "But I know one brother who better not think he can get away with that mess." They all laughed.

Jaden said, "I'm not that kind of brother. Men who beat on women are nothing but cowards to me. When I was nine I saw my next door neighbor's dad hit his mom. The blow was so hard she fell on the concrete and hit her head. There was a gash over her eye and blood flowed out of it. The coward ran because he heard the police coming. That one event left an impression on me for life. I knew I could never treat a woman like that."

Penny replied, "Wow, you were only nine years old and had to be exposed to something like that? I can't stand that type of man."

Nya added, "I feel you on that Penny. A man only has one time then he'll get the Al Green treatment…hot grits."

They all burst into laughter, remembering the story of Al Green. They heard a knock at the door and Penny got up to answer it. She got to the door and saw Jay standing there. She let him in and gave him a friendship hug. She liked Jay and secretly hoped that one day he would get back with Raine. To her, they made the perfect couple. Penny made a gesture to Jay, "Come on in the dining room Jay; we're just talking."

Jay replied, "Okay; hi Mr. Cornelius."

Cornelius looked up from his cup of tea, "Hi, you doing okay?"

"Yes sir and you?"

"I'm doing okay."

Penny walked in, "Daddy you need anything else?"

"No, baby."

"Okay, push the button if you need one of us."

"Okay baby, I will."

They walked into the dining room and Jay greeted Jaden and Nya. He sat at the table with everyone and they continued talking.

The conversation moved away from Raine but continued until close to midnight. Penny was enjoying herself. It was nice to take her mind off of her sister for a while.

As Jay and Jaden were leaving, Penny heard a loud noise and people laughing outside. She went to investigate.

Penny saw Raine with her entourage including Damien. Penny ran out the front door and stood on the porch. Raine came up to the porch while everyone stayed back.

Penny's eyes were sharp and pointed. She was fixated on Raine, "You're drunk and you just got out the hospital. What is wrong with you Raine? Have you lost your mind?"

Raine frowned and pointed at Penny, "So what; I'm having a good time and you just can't stand it."

"I don't mind anyone having a good time; it's just how you do it and who you chose to do it with."

Nya came out on the porch followed by Jaden and Jay. Raine said, "Wow, the gangs all here; hey Jaden." She hugged Jayden, "So, when you gonna marry my stuck up sister?"

"Hi Raine," said Jaden. He stepped to the side and hugged Penny, "Bye, sweetheart. I'll see you tomorrow."

"Okay," said Penny.

Raine just staggered to the next person, "Nya, you like that money I been sending you; you can't tell me you don't?"

Nya stared coldly, "Raine…I haven't received a cent from you. You said you wanted to help us the only way you could, financially, but I have yet to receive anything from you."

"What, that's not true. For the last three months I've been sending you money every week."

Nya folded her arms, "That's not true Raine but maybe you're so high and drunk all the time that you don't even notice." She turned and walked back in the house.

Raine looked at Penny, "No money?"

Penny answered, "None, not a dime."

Raine staggered to Jay, "Hey baby; you missed me?"

Jay eased off of her, "I miss the Raine I use to know. I don't know who you are."

He walked off the porch to his car. Raine and Penny watched him as he got in and drove off. Jay never looked back and Penny believed that was going to be the last time she would see him.

"He'll be back," said Raine. "They all love me. Where's my daddy?"

Penny answered, "Oh no, you're not going in there like this. Daddy is in bad enough shape as it is and he doesn't need to see you like this. If you want to see him, come back...sober."

Raine shouted, "You ain't the boss."

"I have a legal document that says otherwise. Leave now, Raine or I'm calling the police."

Damien came up on the porch and took Raine by the arm, "The police, you'd call the police on me?" She looked at Damien, "She tryna kick me out my own house Damien."

"Come on baby; like I told you before, you're not wanted here anymore. They're all jealous of you." He kissed her on the lips and she kissed him deeply.

Raine left with Damien pulling her by the arm. Penny had tears in her eyes as Raine stared at her. Penny could not let Raine upset their father. He had been through enough.

Nya joined Penny back on the porch as Raine got back in the limo and they all drove off. Nya said, "She just had to make a spectacle of herself."

"Yes, she did."

Chapter 30

Raine woke up the next morning with a severe handover. She remembered having the time of her life opening a restaurant, speaking on the radio and opening two stores in the mall. Most of all, she remembers being thrown off her family's property because she was drunk and high. She remembers how her two sisters and her ex-boyfriend treated her and she wasn't happy about it.

She sat on the side of the bed thinking about Jay and his disappointment in her. She still loved him and there was no denying that. She looked at Damien as he slept and he disgusted her so much that she wanted to vomit. The thought of killing him came to mind again.

She got up and dressed as fast as she good. Today was her hometown concert and she was excited but she had to go visit her daddy. She really wanted to see him and this time, she was going to be sober when she arrived.

***

Raine's limo pulled up in front of the Davis house. Raine could see her father sitting on the porch with Penny. She got out of the limo, adjusted her dress and walked up to the house.

Penny met her before she got to the steps and looked her over. Raine said, "I'm not drunk or high."

Penny stepped to the side and let Raine go by. Raine ran up the steps and hugged her daddy like it was the first time in years she'd seen him.

"Hi Daddy; I missed you so much."

Cornelius hugged her tightly, "Hey baby girl; how you doing?"

She was happy he at least remembered who she was, "I'm doing good, Daddy. I see you're taking in this morning sun. It feels good." Raine pulled a chair over to him and sat down. She was so excited to be sitting with her daddy again. Penny was right about one thing, she did enjoy it more not being under the influence.

Cornelius said, "Yeah baby, there's nothing like a little sun to start the day off right. That's why I love Florida; we get a lot of sunshine here."

"I know that's right, Daddy."

Penny asked, "Is there anything I can get you, Daddy?"

Cornelius answered, "No baby, I'm fine just sitting here with my baby girl."

Penny asked, "Raine, you want anything?"

"Some orange juice if you got any? Hey Penny remember that time when we drank all the orange juice up from Daddy?"

Penny smiled but Cornelius shocked them, "Yeah and I tore both your butts up too."

Penny and Raine looked at each other. The doctors told Penny that Cornelius would lose most of his long-term memory but this incident happened fifteen years ago.

Raine said, "I thought you said the doctors…"

Penny cut her off, "Don't question it; just be happy. I'm just as shocked as you are."

Penny went on in the house and left Raine alone with their father. Raine stood up and hugged him again, "Daddy, I love you so much."

Cornelius smiled, "I love you too, baby. I wish your mother were here to see how much you've grown."

Raine was shocked again. This was the first time she knew of that their father remembered that their mother had passed.

Penny rejoined them and Raine whispered in her ear, "He remembered that momma passed away."

Penny looked surprised at Raine, "He did?"

Raine nodded, "Yes; do you think he's getting his memory back?"

"I certainly hope so." Penny looked at Raine with a serious face, "How are you Raine? I mean really, don't try and sugar coat it."

Raine paused, to give her answer some thought, "I could be better." She looked Penny in the eyes then back to the ground, "Sometimes, I don't know if I'm coming or going. I mean, I love singing but the other things…I just don't know."

Penny put her arm around Raine, "You can always come home."

For the first time that reference didn't anger Raine at all. It was nice to know that despite everything she did and said, her sister still wanted her to come home.

Before she could answer, Damien drove up. He got out the limo and called out, "Raine, we need to go. We have a lot to do before tonight."

Raine smiled at Penny, "Will you come to the concert…please?"

"Yes, I drew the straw to go, so Nya has to stay with Daddy."

"I wish you both could come but I understand. I'll make sure your tickets are at the will call booth."

Penny smiled, "Thanks, I'll see you tonight."

They hugged and Raine left. She sat in her limo quietly thinking about her family and her life. She knew she had to get away from Damien. She had to end her marriage. She wondered what Jay was doing.

Chapter 31

Raine sat in her dressing room waiting for her turn to go on stage. She had opened for major artists for the first three months of the tour but in her hometown she was the star. She would be the last act on stage and she wanted to give her hometown something to remember her by.

Her cell phone rang, "Penny, are you here?"

"Yes, and guess who took Nya's ticket and came with me?"

Raine quickly answered, "Jaden, but I left a ticket for him too."

"No girl; Jaden is here too but Jay is here with us."

Raine smiled and wondered if Penny felt it over the phone, "Really; can I talk to him?"

"Yeah, hold on."

"Hey Raine, I came to see you perform. Give us something to remember baby."

Raine was happy as she could be. She still loved Jay more than anything. She knew inside she wanted him back. The smile on her face lit up the room. After everything she had said and done this man still loved her, and she loved him.

She said, "Hey Jay. I'm so happy you came to my concert. Listen for something really special for you tonight."

"Okay, baby."

Raine continued, "I'm sorry about last night and everything that's happened since I signed that stupid contract."

Raine realized her comment was the first time she referred to her contract as 'stupid'. She was truly feeling the need to get out of the world she felt trapped in.

Jay said, "Raine you are still the most important woman in my life. You might have married another man but I haven't let go. I still believe and I still love you."

Raine was truly happy to hear those words again from the man she thought she'd lost. Now, she heard him say the words that she took for granted when they were together. Hearing them one more time filled her with so much joy that she forgot the pain of living with Damien. She became more daring and decided she was going to tell the world how she truly felt.

"I still love you too, Jay. After the concert I'm going to my house to celebrate with my family and close friends. Will you be there?"

"I don't know baby, your husband is a jerk and I don't want to cause trouble. If he treats you bad in front of me, I won't be able to contain myself."

"Oh, somehow I doubt he'll be there. That's why I'm choosing to do it this way. Jay, I'm leaving him after the show. I can't take it anymore. I'm tired of being battered and beaten. I'm tired of the all the drugs and alcohol. I want my happiness back. Will you help me?"

Jay said quickly, "Yes. I will always be here for you baby. No matter what, we'll get through this together."

Raine was so happy; she didn't know what to do with herself. She believed her sisters would always be there for her but this man had no reason to be there for her at all, but he was. He still loved her and it brought tears of joy to her eyes.

Raine's assistant came in the room, "We're ready."

Raine held up one finger, "I have to go now. It's time for me to come out on stage. I'll see you in a few minutes."

"Knock 'em dead, baby."

"I will, sweetheart."

Raine hung up the phone, got on her knees and bowed her head.

"Father, I have been absent from you. I have not been in your number. You know all that I have done and all that I have suffered. Tonight, I will take the first step out of this life. I will leave my abusive marriage. I will leave the drugs behind. No more alcohol shall cross my lips. I will return to your arms. I know I haven't prayed in months but Father; if you hear a sinner's cry, please hear mine. In your magnificent son Jesus' name I pray...Amen!"

She rose and headed to the stage. This was the moment she had been waiting for since she started her career. She was going to perform in front of all her family and friends in her hometown then celebrate her success at her home with her family. She only had one problem, how to deal with Damien afterwards.

She walked the long winding hallway to the stage with confidence and vigor. This was the moment that she lived for, the time that no one could cause her pain. She was in control and she loved putting on shows for her fans. This one had a special significance for her because it was her hometown. She was going to perform for people she grew up with and loved dearly but most of all, she was going to leave Damien and tell the world who she truly loved. She made up her mind and she was going to do it in the place that she felt most comfortable…on stage.

Her assistant asked, "After the concert, we're going to head straight to the after party at the hotel or are we meeting with the media first? I know you have tons of family and friends here, so we can meet everyone here and then head to the party later. That way anyone who wants to attend can follow us and we can get them into the party."

Raine said "Forget the media. I'm going straight to my party." She stopped and looked at her assistant, "I want to be in my limo by myself. Tell Damien, I'll meet him at the party okay? Also have my limo wait for me on the other side of the building. I know we planned for me to exit the stage on the right but I'll be leaving on the left. Please, please don't share that information with anyone, okay?"

"Yes ma'am."

"Promise me, it could mean my life."

"I promise, Miss Davis; I won't tell it."

Raine trusted her assistant more than anyone in her entourage. She knew that her assistant had suffered through an abusive relationship herself and if anyone understood what Raine was going through it was her assistant.

On several occasions Raine's assistant tried to get her to call the abuse hotline but Raine wouldn't listen. She wouldn't believe that she was being abused. Now she trusted her to keep her escape plan a secret. She was prepared to take the first step.

From the moment Raine stepped on staged she was filled with excitement and love for her occupation. She was a singer and nothing thrilled her more than the performance. From the moment she stepped on stage she got energy from the crowd. That energy encouraged her to give the best that she had to give.

It had been months since she gave a performance without illicit drugs or alcohol in her system. She felt powerful, moving and enthusiastic, like she could do no wrong. Everyone in the arena chanted her name. The arena was louder than it had ever been before.

From time to time she would look to the front row and see her friends and family. She left over 50 tickets for all of them. It did her heart wonders to see Penny smiling and pointing at her like she was proud. After everything they had gone through, she was still her sister.

She dedicated a song to Penny and brought her on stage to help sing it. The two of them sung one of Raine's songs and sent the audience into a frenzy. It was a very emotional moment for the Davis' sisters.

Halfway through the show she made a speech, "I'm so excited to be here tonight to perform for my hometown. I love y'all!" The crowd yelled their love back to her, "This next song is dedicated to a man that I realize that I love more than any man in my life. I know that it won't make some people happy but I'm dedicating this song to you, Jason Thompson, I still love you."

The crowd went crazy. Many of them didn't know that she didn't dedicate the song to her husband but to her ex-boyfriend. No one but the people backstage knew how angry this made her husband. Raine knew it would make him angrier than ever. She didn't care because she made up in her mind that she was leaving him.

Tonight would be the last night she would be Misses Damien Black and she sang her newest number one hit, "I Still Love You" with more power and motivation than ever before. She meant every word and every time she sang the words, 'I still love you', she looked at Jay in the front row. It culminated in a kiss she blew at him at the end of the song.

She breezed through the rest of the show with a smile that wouldn't stop. She knew her fans, family and friends loved every minute of her performance and she loved giving it to them. Over and over she heard her name being called. This was the best performance she ever had. It culminated with the song 'Let it Raine' and fake hundred dollar bills with Raine's face on them raining down from the ceiling. The crowd was at a fever pitch.

When she was ready to go off stage she saw Damien waiting at the side of the stage where she was supposed to exit. She knew her assistant had kept her word and not told anyone. Damien had his arms folded and she knew he was mad and wanted to beat her or possibly kill her.

She held her hands up and yelled, "I will always love you, Florida!"

Raine kicked her shoes into the audience and took a bow. When she came up, she darted off the stage in the opposite direction and asked her security team to take her directly to her limo. They did and before Damien could get to her, she was gone.

She looked out the rear window and saw Damien standing in the parking lot. She knew he was angry but she also knew he wouldn't dare come to her family's home and cause trouble. She directed the driver to take her to her daddy's house.

***

Raine's limo pulled up to the Davis house and she immediately took a deep breath knowing she would be safe. She got out and ran into the house where Nya and her dad where sitting and watching television.

Nya said, "Hey, the concert is over?"

"Yeah girl and I'm in big trouble."

Nya rushed over with concern on her face, "Why?"

Raine paced the floor, holding her forehead in the palm of her hand and looking at Nya. She then looked out the door to see if anyone was there. She said, "I dedicated 'I Still Love You' to Jay and I know Damien is crazy mad. He's gonna kill me, Nya."

"Raine, why would you do that?"

Raine stomped her foot, "I'm tired, Nya. I can't take it anymore." Tears streamed down her face, "I have to get out of this marriage. I have to free myself of him and I can't deny my feeling for Jay anymore. I love him and I'm going to be with him, even if it kills me."

Raine threw herself into her sister's arms. She was scared and in tears. Nya hugged her sister as tightly as she could and the two of them just stood there hugging for what seemed like hours.

Nya said, "Well, he's gonna have to go through the entire Davis clan before that happens and I ain't having it."

Raine smiled. Of all the Davis girls, Nya was the fighter. Penny was the protector and Raine was the baby. Raine said, "I know we haven't been the best of friends or sisters but…but I love you Nya. I'm sorry for everything I have ever said or done to you…okay?"

Nya smiled and hugged her sister even tighter, "No apologies needed girl. I'm the one who was jealous of you for being the baby. That was so stupid of me. Do you forgive me?"

Raine laughed, "Yeah, girl." That's what she wanted to hear and this time she was going to make sure her relationship with her sisters stayed tight. The time for fighting was over. She was going to keep her profession, leave her husband and love her family more than she ever could. Today was going to be the day everything changed for Raine Davis. She promised herself that.

Raine sat down and looked at her dad, "Hey Daddy, You okay?"

Cornelius answered, "I'm fine baby. How was the show?"

Raine smiled again. Her father appeared to be getting better each day, "It was great, Daddy. It was everything I imagined it would be. I only wish you could have been there."

"Next time, baby girl; next time."

"Okay, Daddy."

***

The Davis' home was filled with family and friends for the after party. Damien was blowing up Raine's phone but she refused to answer it. Instead she was enjoying the party at her daddy's house.

Reporters came by her house and wanted to interview her and she told the world who Jay was and that her marriage was over. She knew there was going to be a rocky road for her to change but inside she felt so much better.

Jay wouldn't leave her side and she enjoyed it. For the first time in months, she had fun without being under the influence. She also didn't have to be worried about being beaten. Jay wouldn't raise a hand at her and she knew it. She was having so much fun that she didn't even miss the drugs or alcohol.

As the night went on, people began to leave until it was just Raine, her father, her sisters, Jay and Jaden.

Raine asked Jay in front of everyone, "Jay, can you stay with me tonight?"

Penny jumped in, "Raine you know that's not right. Daddy would not want you with another man, under his roof."

Raine said, "I know Penny but if Jay and Jaden leave, there's no man here if Damien comes. Jay, I know it's a sin for you to be with me and I'm married but can you at least stay here in the house? I'm afraid of what Damien might do if there's no man around."

Jay looked at Penny then back at Raine, "I'll stay here, baby. That jerk won't hurt you anymore."

Jaden added, "I'm staying too. I'm proud of you Raine for standing your ground and I'm here to help defend you. That coward won't get his hands on you."

Raine smiled and Penny chimed in again, "I guess you're right. It would be nice for a man, or two, to be here in case he does show up."

Nya said, "Dang, I wish my man were here."

Everyone laughed and Penny added, "Yeah, if Carlton were here he'd put some of that military training on Damien's butt."

They all laughed. Raine took Jay by the hand and lead him to her room. She smiled, "I guess you can't sleep in here with me."

Jay replied, "No, but I'll be in the living room. No one will hurt you. I promise."

Raine smiled and handed him a pillow and a blanket. Secretly, she wanted him to stay in the bedroom with her but she knew that wasn't going to work. It would be disrespectful to her daddy and she didn't want to do that.

Jay went into the living room, leaving Raine in her bedroom alone. She sat on the bed in deep thought. Her train of thought was broken by Penny, "It's going to be okay, baby girl."

Raine hugged her big sister. She believed it would be okay.

Penny reiterated, "It's going to be okay."

"I know," said Raine. "I'm so glad to be back. I love you, Penny." She looked solemnly into Penny's eyes, "You're not a twenty-seven year old washed up has been either. You're the best singer I know."

Penny smiled, "Wow…that must have taken a lot for you to say."

Raine smiled back, "Not really. I knew it all along. You're my big sister and you taught me. You have to be the best."

Nya walked in the room and joined the hugging party. For the first time in a long while the sisters felt like sisters again. Raine knew the last six months were mostly her fault and she let the fame, drugs and alcohol consume her but she trusted her sisters to help her change her life. The only thing she worried about was the contract.

She didn't want out of the contract but she was afraid of what the signing in blood meant. This was a topic she felt she had to keep to herself. She couldn't tell her sisters about signing a contract in blood because she feared that if they found out, it could mean their lives.

Penny said, "I love you guys."

Nya said, "I love you guys too."

Raine said, "You know I have to show y'all up, I love you guys the most!"

They all laughed, like true sisters.

Chapter 32

Damien paced the floor of the hotel penthouse suite. He was angry and couldn't wait to get his hands on his wife. He was going to make her pay for embarrassing him in front of the world. Not only did she dedicate and perform a love song to another man at her hometown concert but she then told the world in an interview afterwards, how much she truly loved and missed him.

The knock on the door was his friend Don. "Hey Don, what's up?"

Don came in shaking his head, "Man, she's gone overboard now. I can't believe she dedicated that song to her ex in front of everybody. Then she goes on an interview and tells everyone how much she truly loves him. That's nothing but disrespect."

The comment made Damien even madder than before, "She's gonna pay. Mark my words; her little black behind is going to pay."

Don asked, "What you planning?"

Damien pulled out his Glock and showed it to Don, "I'm going to go find her and she won't be dedicating any songs to anyone else. Trust me on that!"

"Whoa man, you need to take a step back here and think about what you're doing. You're talking premeditated murder."

"I'm talking revenge, my brother. If she wants out of the marriage then I'm going to give it to her."

Don pleaded, "Look Damien, you're my boy and all but I can't let you do this. It's a mistake, a big mistake. You know what they will do to you."

"I don't care Don. She disrespected me and I'm going to make sure she doesn't disrespect me ever again." Damien looked coldly into Don's eyes. He wasn't going to change his mind. Raine had disrespected him by dedicating that song to Jay and then leaving the concert without him. He knew she was in his arms and he was going to kill her and him too if he got in the way. Nothing was going to stop him.

Don continued to plead, "Dude, they will kill you. You might succeed in killing Raine but they will kill you. Then what will you gain?"

"I'll have my satisfaction. Anyway, I'm going to take her out and then get on the first plane out of here. They won't find me where I'm going. I won't even tell you."

Don shook his head, "Damien, my brother, they will find you. They have people and resources everywhere.

You know they run the entire world not just the music industry man. They'll find you."

Damien looked at Don, "You'd better get out of here before I consider taking you out." He walked up to Don, "Don't tell anyone about my plan or I'll hunt you down, got it?" Damien took a couple of steps backward and drank a glass of bourbon. "I know you have a thing for LaJuan too. If you run and tell her, I'll kill you." He winked at him.

Don quickly replied, "Yeah man, I got it."

Damien knew Don wouldn't tell a soul because he was afraid of Damien. They knew each other for years and if anyone knew what Damien was capable of, it was Don.

Damien stepped back, "Good, now go so you won't be implicated in any of this."

Don quickly left the room and Damien continued to pace the floor. He knew where Raine was and he knew she wasn't going to come back to the penthouse.

He gathered his things and put them in his rental car. He wanted to kill Raine and anyone who got in his way. Just in case Don did run and tell LaJuan, he was going to take a bus to another city and then take a plane. He needed to get out of town quickly before the news of Raine's death broke.

He would have to take a couple of planes to lose the men in suits but he was prepared. He believed he had enough cash on him and hidden away to get away with it.

Chapter 33

Nya laid awake in her bed thinking. She remembered all the fun times she use to have with her sisters and now she prayed they would have that life again; only this time she would make every effort to ensure she got along with Raine. She wasn't worried about her relationship with Penny; they always got along for the most part. She decided she would not let petty jealously come between her and her baby sister any longer.

The ringing phone broke her silence. She knew who it had to be and she quickly reached for the phone, accidently knocking it to the floor. She rushed to grab it before it stopped ringing, "Hello…sorry I dropped the phone, hello."

Carlton answered, "Hey sweetheart; I thought I was going to miss you."

Nya fell back on the pillow, smiling, "No baby, I was just excited to hear the phone rang. I knew it had to be you this early in the morning."

"Yeah, we're getting ready to head out on patrol so I wanted to call you while I had a few minutes. How was everything last night? I know Raine was in town for her concert. Did it go well?"

Nya sighed, "It went better than expected. She wants out of her marriage. She even got on stage and told the world she still loves Jay. She dedicated 'I Still Love You' to him. Her husband has got to be enraged."

Carlton snickered, "She did that? Oh man, I know he's fuming. From what you guys have said, I would be careful and don't leave her alone."

"She's not. We have Jay and Jaden here, so we have capable men in the house in case that jack…"

"Now baby, you know you better."

Nya sighed, "Okay, but you know what I wanted to say."

Carlton said, "Yeah, but you're a good Christian woman. Don't let the thought of him bring you down, baby."

Nya smiled again. She only got to spend one day with Carlton before he shipped out to Iraq but that was all they needed to reunite. They rediscovered the love they had for each other and now they were making it work from a long distance. Nya only had three more months to endure and he would back in the states.

Nya said, "I won't baby. I miss you."

"I miss you too, Nya. When I come back, I'm being assigned to the Washington DC area."

Nya sat up quickly, "What... how are we going to make it work?"

Carlton said, "Oh, I don't know, maybe we should just... get married."

Nya eased backed down on the pillow, "Carlton did you just propose to me?"

"I think so." The phone was quiet then Carlton continued, "You see Nya, we may have reunited our relationship but we've known each other since high school. I don't know about you but I feel like we should never have broken up. This time, I want to lock it down, make it permanent, you and me, forever. So will you marry me?"

Nya smiled so hard she couldn't talk. She, of course, wanted to marry him but being proposed to over the phone was something she never expected. She thought, *'Well, I never expected to be in a long distance relationship either. What the heck.'*

She answered, "Yes, Carlton, I'll marry you. Where's my ring?"

Carlton said, "Look under your mattress."

Nya jumped up and threw the mattress off the bed. She found a ring box with an engagement ring in it. She didn't know what to say.

"Carlton, how did you do that?"

"I had that ring with me since we were dating. We broke up before I could give it to you. When I was at your house that day after church, I tipped in your room and put it there. It was my hope that we would get to this point and I would ask you to marry me. I didn't want you to be without a ring."

Nya said, "Awe honey, that's so sweet. It's a good thing I didn't flip my mattresses yet."

Carlton replied, "Baby, I have to head out now. I'll call later today when we return."

Tears formed in Nya's eyes. She didn't want him to go but she understood, "Okay baby. I'll talk to you later."

"Bye, sweetheart."

"Bye honey." After hanging up she admired her engagement ring. Now, it was her turn to show Penny her ring. She was so happy that the loud crashing sound from the front of the house almost went unheard. She dashed to the front of the house. Her happiness quickly turned to fear.

Chapter 34

Penny laid awake in her bed thinking. The events of the last day was what she had prayed would happen. Her sister, Raine had seen the light and was coming home. Even though she wasn't going to be physically home she was going to leave the drugs, alcohol and most importantly Damien behind. She was headed in the right direction. Now, the hard part was keeping him away from her and keeping her focused on changing.

The buzzer alerted her that her dad needed care. It was her night to take care of him. She didn't mind because Nya carried more of the load than she did. She had grown accustomed to the irritating sound so the second she heard it, she was up and headed to his room.

She asked, "Daddy, what's wrong, what can I get for you?"

Cornelius was afraid, "Baby, something bad is going to happen."

Penny comforted him, "Daddy, it was just a bad dream. I'm right here so go back to sleep. I'll be right here."

Cornelius said, "Honey, you are my first born and I love you so much. I remember when you were a little girl, how you'd run around outside playing with all your friends. You could always make friends so easily. I think you got that quality from your mother."

Penny marveled at how clearly her father was thinking. She thought, *'He's really coming around. I think he's going to get all of his memory back now. Praise the Lord.'*

Cornelius asked, "Baby, can I ask you something?"

Penny smiled, "Sure Daddy, you can ask me anything."

Cornelius' face turned serious, "Would you really die for your sisters?"

Penny was shocked by the question. She would in an instant die for him and both of her sisters but she didn't know why he asked that question.

Penny answered, "Daddy, without a doubt, I would die for you and my sisters. I love my family and you guys are all I have. There's nothing on Earth more important than family."

Cornelius dropped his head to the side, "I love you, baby." He closed his eyes as if he were going to sleep.

Penny said, "Daddy…Daddy are you okay?"

"I'm fine, sweetheart."

Penny was so focused on her father that she almost didn't hear the loud crashing sound coming from the front of the house. Before she could leave, her father grabbed her arm, "I love you, baby."

She stared at him for an instant, then ran up front to see what was happening. She saw Nya frozen in place, soon she did the same.

Chapter 35

Raine woke up to a loud thunderous noise from the front of the house. She feared the worst was about to happen. It took a minute to gather herself then run into the living room area. Her sisters were blocking the entrance from the bedrooms to the living room. Once Raine got between them she understood why.

Damien was standing in the living room on top of the fallen front door. Apparently, he kicked the door in and was now pointing a gun at Raine's beloved Jay.

Her heart dropped. He had gone crazy. She had pushed him completely over the top and now he was going to kill the man she loved more than anyone else.

She squeezed between Penny and Nya and pleaded, "Damien no! Please don't do this."

Damien stared coldly at her, "Come here Raine."

Raine was frozen in her tracks. Penny put her arms on Raine's shoulder to hold her back. Raine said, "Don't shoot him Damien, please. I beg you."

Damien replied, "I won't, if you get over here now."

Penny's grip tightened on Raine. Raine looked at her with tears in her eyes, "I have to Penny."

Raine knew Penny didn't want her to go but Raine loved Jay too much to just watch him die in front of her. She was willing to sacrifice herself to save him.

Jay shouted, "Raine don't!"

Raine turned and pulled out of Penny's grip. Penny shouted, "Raine!"

Damien moved the gun away from Jay's head and pointed it at Raine. Penny moved toward her sister and pushed her to the side and on top of Jay. Both Jay and Raine fell to the side and on the couch.

The sound of the gun exploding in the morning air was louder than anything Raine ever heard in her life. Her father cried out from his room, "Nooooo…" She knew he hurt badly because he couldn't help his daughters.

Then Nya screamed. Raine wanted to scream but Jay turned her over quickly to put himself between her and Damien. Jay loved her and he meant it when he said he would protect her.

Jaden and Damien fought and the gun went off, again. Raine jumped at the sound. She couldn't see anything because Jay was on top of her, blocking anything from happening to his woman.

She heard punching and screaming, then another shot went off and the gun fell to the ground. Jay moved to get it, turned and fired out the front door opening.

Raine held her hands over her ears and jumped at each shot. She was terrified and crying for all of them. The shooting stopped but Raine didn't move her hands from her ears. She expected more but prayed for less. Now the room was filled with screams, sobbing and crying.

Raine screamed and jumped when Jay touched her by the arm. She looked at him, jumped up and grabbed him so hard that she almost went through him. She heard Nya whimpering behind her. She saw Jaden's body lying on the ground not moving. She gasped. She looked at Jay, "No, please say he's not…" She couldn't finish the sentence.

Jay said softly, "He's dead, Raine."

Raine sobbed and cried, "No, please no." She turned to look for Penny. She knew Penny would hate her now but it was worse than that. She'd rather Penny hate her for the rest of her life then to see what she was seeing now.

Penny's body lay motionless on the floor. Nya knelt over her holding Penny's hand and she was covered with blood. Raine screamed, "Noooooo, not my sister! Noooo!" She pushed Jay away and quickly crawled over to Penny's motionless body and grabbed her tightly. Nya rubbed her back continuing to whimper. Jay tried to comfort her but she wasn't having it.

Raine was shaking Penny's body vigorously; hoping she could wake her from a deep sleep. It was to no avail. Raine's big sister was gone. She had taken the road to Heaven to join their mother.

It was Raine's worst nightmare. The paramedics and police arrived. They tried to pull Raine away from her sister but she refused. Everyone decided to let her have her moment. Reporters and fans filled the street in front of Raine's home. This was one time that she hated being in the limelight.

Nya put her arm around her sister, "Raine, we have to go see about Daddy. Come on baby girl come with me, please. I can't do this without you."

Raine was still in tears but she eased away from Penny's body and into Nya's arms. Together they both went to tell their father what happened. Somehow they knew… he already knew.

Chapter 36

The news of the shootings at the Davis house filled the airwaves all day. The evening quickly approached and LaJuan was very angry. Damien was on the run and thought he was going to get away but she would handle him later. First, she needed to handle Don. She believed he knew what Damien was planning and purposely didn't tell her. For that, she had to make him pay dearly.

She received a reliable tip on where Don was hiding out. She knew he had an old girlfriend in the city. She waited in the alley down the street from her apartment. She called his cell number knowing he would answer.

Don said, "Hey LaJuan, did you hear what happened at Raine's parent's house?"

LaJuan answered, "Yeah, and I have it on good authority that you knew all about it beforehand. You let me down for the last time, Don. For that you have to pay."

Don pleaded, "No, LaJuan I swear, I didn't know anything about it."

LaJuan shouted, "Liar. Don't think hiding in your old girlfriend's apartment will save you either."

The line went dead. She knew he would be running out soon. If he tried to get in his vehicle he would find that it wouldn't start. She had taken care of that. She also had some old friends who would ensure he would run toward her so she just leaned against the wall and waited.

Soon, she heard the pitter patter of feet running in her direction. She smiled. It was times like these she enjoyed. Behavioral analysts would liken her to a Hedonistic serial killer who is driven by the thrill, lust, sex, pleasure or as in LaJuan's case, financial gain brought on by murder.

The footsteps drew closer to LaJuan and she readied herself for the climax. He was now close enough. She stepped from behind the building and aimed at his head. She smiled, seeing the fear in his eyes, and pulled the trigger. He never had a chance to even beg.

One shot to the forehead was all it took. Don was dead before he hit the ground. LaJuan's mission was complete.

Chapter 37

It had been two days since Penny and Jaden were shot to death in her living room. She hadn't said a word to reporters who were constantly standing on her front lawn. She hadn't said a word to family or close friends who came to visit. Raine only spoke quietly with her father and Nya.

The rain eased down across the city and it was dark and gloomy. Raine liked the weather on this day because it fit her mood. She felt dark and gloomy inside so it didn't bother her that it was dark and gloomy outside. Nya found her on the back porch, "Those reporters just won't leave."

Raine didn't turn around, "No, they'll stay there until I come out. They relish in misery. They have no desire to allow me to grieve. They only want a story." She stood up and looked at Nya, "And, I'm not going to give them one. They can stay out there and rot for all I care."

Nya snickered, "That's my girl."

Raine said, "Nya, I brought all of this on our family. If I had stayed here, finished college and got a nine to five like everyone else, Penny would still be here. She would be getting ready to get married and I would be the maid of honor."

Nya replied, "Excuse me, I don't think so, baby."

Raine laughed, "You know it's true. Come on now."

They hadn't laughed since that tragic day but now they were dealing with the pain. The two of them found a way to end their differences and get along. They were the only two Davis women left. Their father had another relapse the day after Penny died and was in the hospital again.

Raine said, "Nya, I will get you that money. I have plenty and I surely don't need it all for myself. You can use it to get Daddy into a home since you're moving to DC."

Nya looked out into the rain. She wasn't smiling, "I decided not to go to DC."

"What? You can't do that. Carlton will be there. Don't put your relationship on hold."

Nya said, "I won't be putting it on hold, Raine. We will still be in our relationship. It will just be long distance. Our relationship is surviving Iraq, it can survive DC. All I ask is that you come home every chance you get. Daddy will need both his daughters around, as much as possible."

Raine said calmly, "I will, Nya. If it's one thing I have learned from all of this is to never, ever forsake my family. I will be here every chance I get, I promise you that. Besides with Damien out of the picture, I imagine my life being much better. I might be working hard but I'll be more in control of what I do. I will be home."

Nya replied, "Sounds like a good plan, baby girl."

Raine smiled, "Besides with Jay by my side, you know I'll be doing the right thing from now on. He won't let me be bad."

Nya laughed, "I know that's right. I love Jay. He's a good guy. I guess we both have good men now."

Raine said, "Yeah, we do. Well it's time to fight this crowd and go see Daddy."

"Yeah, let's do it."

Chapter 38

It was the day before her sister's funeral was scheduled to be held. Her assistant and new manager encouraged her to speak publicly to the media. Initially, Raine didn't want to speak to them but she decided for her fans sake that she would go ahead with it.

Raine asked Nya to be by her side on the podium when she spoke. She wanted the comfort of her sister while she spoke. Nya easily agreed.

Raine came out to the podium and looked over the room. The reporters were all fixed on her as she stepped up to speak. She started, "Tomorrow I will lay my sister to rest. The last week has been difficult for me and my family but at the same time we have become closer than we ever have. My sister, Nya…" She turned and pointed at Nya, "and I, are the best of friends now. That's a statement that I am happy to make."

"Now, comes the time when I need to decide my future. In the last 18 months I have loss my mother and my sister, two people that I love so much. The loss of my sister is a high price that I had to pay to achieve the success that I have. Therefore, I have decided to leave the music industry." Raine's manager and Nya were puzzled. Clearly they didn't know Raine was quitting.

The cameras began to flash and reporters started to ask questions all at once. Raine motioned for quiet, "For the sake of my many fans, I will resume my tour and complete it. Afterwards, I will quit singing and return home to take care of my father. I accept any legal issues that may arise from this decision but it is one that I feel I must make at this time."

"I want to let everyone at Fresh City Records know that I appreciate all they have done for my career. I thank them so much for their concern and help with the funeral arrangements for my sister and my sister's fiancée. They have been great but I just can't continue with this career knowing that my previous decisions cost my sister her life."

"I cannot take any questions at this time and I thank all of you for allowing me to speak this morning. Thank you."

She quickly turned and walked off stage followed by her sister and her entourage. She heard her new manager start to speak to the reporters behind her but she didn't stop to look. She just wanted to get home and be with all of her family, especially her father.

Chapter 39

It was a dark alley where police were called out. There was a body of a man approximately 30 years old, lying in the alley with a needle stuck in his arms. It was an apparent drug overdose. The officer looked in the man's wallet and his driver's license said his name was 'Damien Black'.

He looked in the man's wallet and found a business card belonging to a 'LaJuan Craig'. The officer called the number and asked Ms. Craig to come to the scene.

LaJuan made it to the scene and identified the body as that of Damien Black. She left the scene and got in her car.

She made a phone call and when the voice answered she said, "Yes, I've identified the body and I'm headed back now. How should I proceed in handling Raine?"

The voice answered, "You are to do no harm to Raine. We do not have permission to harm her or her family."

LaJuan was upset, "But she broke our…"

"Do you hear me? Do no harm to Raine Davis or her family." The phone went dead and LaJuan understood her orders.

It took 30 minutes to drive outside the city limits and to the large building that sat in the middle of nowhere. LaJuan went inside as if she had been there many times before.

She went down the long hallway to a small room where a man in a dark suit stood guard. She didn't acknowledge him; she just walked inside the room.

Once inside, the man in the room sitting in the chair jumped up and pleaded with her, "LaJuan please help me. Get me out of here. I promise, I'll make things right. Please."

LaJuan as cold as a winter's day in Minnesota responded, "You really thought you could get away with this?"

"LaJuan, we had fun together remember? Remember that day when Raine caught us in bed? We can be an item. I will make everything right. I promise Raine will keep singing and I'll keep her happy, just don't kill me."

LaJuan laughed a wicked, eerie sound, "You don't get it do you?" She laughed some more while Damien stared at her perplexed.

She calmly walked to the door, opened it and looked back at Damien. She said, "Honey…you're already dead."

At the sound of the door closing the floor became translucent. Beneath Damien was a fiery, wicked place. The floor disappeared and Damien fell down into the deep pit of fire.

The guard smiled and LaJuan continued her hideous laugh. LaJuan took the guards arm and they both walked away from the door and out of the building still hearing Damien cry out for his soul.

Chapter 40

Raine stood by her sister's grave dressed in an immaculate red dress. She was beautiful. She refused to wear black to her sister's funeral because she believed that if anyone went to Heaven, it was Penny. She wanted to be bright, even a tad bit happy for her sister.

Her head was down, saddened by the loss of another great woman in her life. Eighteen months before, she lost her mother and now her oldest sister was gone, taken from her by her abusive husband. She didn't shed a tear when she found out that Damien was found dead.

The songstress was singing one of Penny's favorite hymns and it touched everyone, including Raine. Penny use to sing that song all the time and whenever Raine heard it, she thought of her sister. She wanted this to be the last time she heard that song because it was just too painful for her to hear.

Raine felt a strong arm take its place around her neck and she instantly fell into it. Her body responded as if the arm belonged there. She knew it was Jay. He held her and didn't say a word. That was his way. He was a man of few words but he knew when to just comfort his woman. He knew when to talk to her and what to say to her to get her to understand. She should have listened to him months ago but that decision she will always regret.

In hindsight, Raine couldn't understand how she allowed herself to marry Damien. How could she have made such a mistake? It was a mistake that costs her the life of her sister and her sister's fiancée. She knew inside, Nya blamed her but to her credit she didn't show it.

Raine was happy Nya was being strong but she couldn't. She blamed herself for all the pain that was caused to her family. Jay broke her concentration.

Jay finally whispered, "We need to go now, sweetheart."

She didn't want to go but she knew he was right. She looked up at him with pleading eyes. He said a thousand times that he forgave her for her choices but she felt he would never really forgive her, no one really would. Part of her didn't believe that a man's love could be so strong that it would forgive her for her actions.

She turned and walked away with him. In the distanced, she saw Nya sitting in the limo. Carlton had been able to return from Iraq and was sitting with Nya. She was happy Nya found love. She wanted her to be happy.

As the limo slowly left the grave site, Raine swore she saw Penny standing in the distance smiling and waving. She knew it was her imagination. She knew it was only what she wanted to see.

Back at the house, Cornelius sat in his wheelchair staring at the walls. It pained Raine's heart to see him this way. She put her arms around him and squeezed him tightly. She even managed a smile.

She looked over at Nya who smiled in her direction. Carlton sat next to her, holding her hand.

Raine stood up and calmly walked over to Nya. She hesitated for a second and then hugged Nya. Nya responded in kind. Raine felt the rest of their family and friends staring happily at them. In the midst of all the pain there was joy that the remaining Davis sisters were hugging each other.

Nya said, "I've been thinking Raine; I don't think you should give up your music career. You love singing and it's your job. Give up the sins but don't give up singing."

"I don't believe my heart is in it Nya. My decisions cost me my sister's life. How could I go back out there and sing now?"

Nya took her hand, "Do you honestly believe that Penny didn't want you to sing? She loved your singing. It was the other stuff that she had the problem with. She didn't want you hooking up with Damien because she knew he was bad news."

Pastor Henderson came over and put his arm around Raine, "Baby, I'm hearing this conversation and I just need to add my two cents. Your sister here is right. There's nothing wrong with you singing. Singing is not a sin. You know in your heart the things that you've done that are a sin. Eliminate those things and keep singing. It wouldn't hurt to sing some for the Lord either."

Raine managed a smile. In her heart she believed they were right. Penny never wanted her to stop singing; she didn't want her around Damien. She was right about that. Damien was a bad influence. He got her a contract but he abused her regularly and introduced her to drugs and alcohol.

Nya said, "Don't quit, Raine. If you had told me before the press conference, I would have told you the same thing. There are a lot of people out there depending on you and your music. Keep going with it but leave the alcohol and stuff behind. Pastor Henderson has even confirmed there's nothing wrong with singing."

Raine smiled, "I don't know if I'm strong enough to keep it going."

Nya smiled back at her, "You're strong enough. You are my baby sister and a Davis woman. I believe you have the character to achieve great things. You just have to stand firm on your belief in God. Keep him at the forefront and you will be fine."

Raine dropped her head and stepped back, "Okay Pastor, Nya, you're right. Even if I did choose to sing rhythm and blues for the world, I should have kept Jesus first in my life."

Cornelius said, "Raine, your profession is singing but you stand for Jesus. Keep him first and all things will work out for his glory."

Raine and Nya both looked at each other. They were happy to hear their father speak so eloquently again. It was the first words he spoke since that dreadful day a week ago. Raine believed in her heart that Jesus was speaking to her.

She proclaimed, "I will Daddy and I am going to put a gospel song on every CD I make from now on. Furthermore, I am going to sing a gospel song at every concert. It might cost me some fans but I don't care because I'm going to stand like my sister stood, on the name of Jesus Christ!"

Raine's new manager shouted, "Yes!" He pulled out his phone and started to dial a number. Raine just laughed, "I think I made someone in the room very happy. What y'all think?"

For the first time in months there was a feeling of joy and happiness in the Davis home without the impending threat of harm. The prominent family suffered the loss of two of its members but love was back in the air.

***

Nya and Carlton got married and had three kids of their own. Cornelius stayed with Nya and Carlton in DC until Carlton left the military and they all returned to Florida where they lived for the rest of their lives.

Ten years after Penny's death Cornelius went home to be with the Lord. He never completely healed from his strokes but he recovered from his state of depression and enjoyed time with his two daughters, their husbands and his grandchildren.

Raine finished her tour and started working on a gospel CD that would make its way to number one on the charts. She would continue her music career with multiple gold and platinum CDs and too many number one songs to count.

She also married Jay and they had three sons who later formed a music group of their own. Raine never used drugs or had a drink of alcohol again.

From the Author

Domestic violence has been a problem for centuries everywhere. My grandmother suffered in silence as did many others. Today we still have people who are suffering in silence from domestic violence.

In my blog I wrote that black women are murdered at a rate two and a half times greater than white women. Any women abused or murdered is never good but as a black man I am truly saddened by that statistic.

We have to take a stand and stop the violence. We can't turn a blind eye any longer. Here are some ways that we can help those trapped in an abusive relationship.

Plan for your safety. Contact the National Domestic Violence Hotline at 1-800-799-7233. This organization can give you helpful information to help you plan your exit.

Contact your local domestic violence outreach organization. These organizations can help you to determine the best way to assist the person you feel is being abused or if you are the person being abuse they can provide excellent guidance on what you should do next.

Attend a domestic violence support group. You will be surprise to find out that others are suffering or have suffered the same or worse than you. Go out and talk to others who have survived. Their advice can be helpful in getting you or someone you know out of an abusive relationship.

As you can see in Standing Firm anyone can find themselves in an abusive relationship. Raine simply wanted to be a star. However, her desire to be famous was so strong that she sacrificed her moral character to attain it. Once she did she slipped into an abusive relationship then an abusive marriage.

Once she was in it she began giving the excuses that many of us have heard. She told her sister Nya, that she fell during rehearsal and bruised her shoulder. She blamed herself for Damien's anger. She told LaJuan that she was not being abused.

It wasn't long before Raine turned to other ways to deal with her abuse. She began to drink heavily then abuse drugs.

Raine was blessed to have Penny as her sister. Penny was determined to never give up on her sister. She knew what was going on with Raine but she realized that she couldn't do anything until Raine wanted to leave. Once she did Penny was there for her no matter what insults Raine had thrown at her in the past.

A strong family support system is necessary to help the person being abused and Raine had that. Her family was always there for her but Raine had to realize she needed them. Once she realized that she had to get out that abusive relationship her family and friends provided the necessary support to help her get out.

Standing Firm is a fictional novel but someone out there this minute is being abused. If you know of someone who is in an abusive relationship please do something to help.

Let's make a difference now!

Be blessed

Gerald C. Anderson, Sr.